Also by Valerie and Ralph Carnes • THE NEW HUMANITIES

Bodysculpture

WEIGHT TRAINING FOR WOMEN

BY **Valerie and Ralph Carnes**

Photography by Ralph Carnes

SIMON AND SCHUSTER · NEW YORK

COPYRIGHT © 1978 BY VALERIE CARNES AND RALPH CARNES
ALL RIGHTS RESERVED
INCLUDING THE RIGHT OF REPRODUCTION
IN WHOLE OR IN PART IN ANY FORM
PUBLISHED BY SIMON AND SCHUSTER
A DIVISION OF GULF & WESTERN CORPORATION
SIMON & SCHUSTER BUILDING
ROCKEFELLER CENTER
1230 AVENUE OF THE AMERICAS
NEW YORK, NEW YORK 10020
PHOTOGRAPHS BY RALPH CARNES
DESIGNED BY EVE METZ
MANUFACTURED IN THE UNITED STATES OF AMERICA
2   3   4   5   6   7   8   9   10

LIBRARY OF CONGRESS CATALOGING IN PUBLICATION DATA

CARNES, VALERIE.
  BODYSCULPTURE.

  1. REDUCING EXERCISES.   2. WEIGHT LIFTING.
3. EXERCISE FOR WOMEN.   4. REDUCING DIETS.   I. CARNES,
RALPH L., JOINT AUTHOR.   II. TITLE.
RA781.6.C37   613.7'1   78-17269

ISBN 0-671-23058-1

Technical Adviser for Photography: J. William Tinney
Nautilus machines courtesy of Supernautilus, Houston, Texas
Dynamics machines courtesy of the Omega Health Club, Houston,
Texas

To Arthur Jacobson,
who is thin but not naturally so,
and
to Gordon R. Dickson,
who told us to stop talking and start writing

ACKNOWLEDGMENTS

We owe an obvious debt to all the bodybuilders, from Sandow to Schwarzenegger, who have kept the sport alive and who have made their own unique contributions to the field. They have provided inspiration to thousands of people down through the years. Without them, there would be no *Bodysculpture*.

We offer special thanks to Ms. Rhondi St. James, president of the Michael St. James Agency in Houston, and to makeup artist Ms. Victoria Bradburry for providing makeup and hair styling for Valerie's photographs.

Thanks also are due to Ms. Leota Pilgrim, executive secretary extraordinary, who has helped us immeasurably in keeping the manuscript, its multiple copies, and its interminable mailings both on time and correct.

We are also deeply indebted to our friend and agent, Dominick Abel, for providing wise counsel at the beginning and true friendship at the end.

Also, there could be no better editor than Jon Segal, whose advice and perceptiveness were consistently sustaining throughout the production of the manuscript.

CONTENTS

Introduction

For almost a century, women have been deprived of the benefits of exercise with weights as a means of losing unwanted fat, improving health, and sculpturing the shape of the body. Some of the myths that have kept women away from weights are:

- "Weightlifting is only for men."
- "Women are inherently weak creatures, and shouldn't do exercises that call for strength."
- "Working out with weights produces grotesque, bulging muscles."
- "Weightlifting will lower your sexuality in the eyes of men."
- "Weightlifting will make you strong, and men don't like strong women."
- "Everybody knows about those female jocks."

The truth, of course, is that there is nothing grotesque, unsexy, or unfeminine about those lean, smooth-skinned, lovely girls in the health club ads on television. You know, the ones who are forever running along the beach into the sunset. What the ads don't tell you is that these girls have been working out with weights. That's right. The fancy chrome exercise machines shown in the ads are simply mechanical means of performing isotonic exercises: in short, lifting weights. (The health clubs hesitate to call it weightlifting because they fear it might scare business away.)

Let us say it right out front: there is no method known to mankind that will burn fat faster, shape a body easier, drop excess weight more efficiently, and build up stamina more effectively than weight training. *There is no way you can do a more effective job in a short amount of time than by weight training.* In fact, weight training is the ultimate democratic exercise. Your muscles will tell you when you are doing the exercises correctly. You can do them in less than an hour at home at a bare minimum of expense. The effects are quick and constructive.

By following the programs outlined in this book, you can get rid of excess fatty weight, thin down your waist and hips, maintain your health, and be able to wear what you want to, all in the shortest time possible. We call our system Bodysculpture because women—even more easily than men—can use the exercises developed by bodybuilders to shape themselves into the appearance they want. Valerie did it, and her story is told in this book. You can do it, and we want to help you try. You have nothing to lose but your excess baggage and nothing to gain but the body you want.

CHAPTER 1

Bodysculpture: Setting It All in Perspective

You've heard all the publicity, you've seen the articles in the magazines, and you are almost convinced that there may really be something to this idea of Bodysculpture, but you probably have some questions, some misgivings, and some fears. After all, the whole idea of weight training for women is relatively new to everybody, especially to you, and the notion that you can sculpt your body to the shape you want is almost too good to be true. You're right. It is *almost* too good to be true, but it *is* true, and because of it you will be a different person in a short time.

First, what is "weight training"? What will it do for you? And what will it do to you? Let's answer the last question first by talking about what weight training will *not* do to women. That's what most women seem to be concerned about.

Weight training will *not* make you have big, bulging muscles like the guys in the movie *Pumping Iron*. Unless you want to gorge yourself with mineral supplements, protein supplements, massive doses of anabolic steroids, and a 7,000-calorie-per-day diet, you as a woman simply cannot and will not grow huge muscles. It doesn't matter what kind of exercise program you go into, it can't and won't happen; the genes are wrong, the hormones are wrong, the weight distribution is wrong, and the skeletal musculature is wrong. Females have slimmer and lighter muscles than males. Female musculature responds to strenuous exercise by toning up, strengthening, and leaning out. Male musculature responds to exactly the same kind of exercise by becoming larger. It's all in the genes and the hormones, not in the exercise. So don't worry about it. The myth that weights will make your muscles huge is just that.

What will weight training do *for* you?

- It will tone up your muscles quickly, efficiently, and with lasting results.
- It will allow you to concentrate on improving particular body areas (legs, arms, waist, etcetera) in a way that no other form of exercise can do.
- It will allow you to *shape* your body, literally to *sculpt* your body, both overall and segmentally.
- It will condition your entire body, strengthen all of your bodily functions, reduce the possibility of hernia, back strain, joint problems, stiffness, and a host of other problems directly related to being weak and out of shape.
- It will make you strong as no other form of exercise can. Consequently, it will rescue you from the old myth about feminine weakness.
- It will make you feel terrific all the time.

There is no mystery as to how weight training works. What we are talking about has been proven scientifically and has been tested in bodybuilding gyms for the last fifty years. Look at the record: when soldiers returned from World War II, weight training was implemented in rehabilitation programs as the best means for building the strength necessary to enable men with disabling wounds to overcome their handicaps.

When Karate experts from the Japan Karate Association were asked in an early issue of *Samurai* magazine how power in the punches and kicks could be developed, they prescribed weight training.

When professional football teams want to add strength to the line, they put the team into the weightlifting gym.

Whether an athlete wants to regain health, build muscular strength, heal injuries, increase endurance, or lose fat, weight training is universally recommended by the top coaches all over the United States.

When ordinary people want to lose a few pounds, shape up, and regain their vitality, they turn to weight training without knowing it: they join health clubs, *all of which build their programs around exercise machines which are nothing more than mechanical means of lifting weights*.

It is one thing to know what the athletes do. But you want to know what the training routine of the Los Angeles Rams has to do with the woman who has been told by her doctor that she has to lose ten pounds. Or the woman who has just this morning found out that she can't get into last year's winter clothes (or worse: that most of her hangs out of last year's bikini!). Or the woman who just doesn't feel good anymore.

Let's start at the beginning, with the muscles themselves. Please bear with us for a little while, because things may sound a bit technical at first. They're not, really, because there's no mystery to any of this. Besides, you'll make faster progress if you know what's happening and why.

Your body moves through the action of the skeletal muscles, the ones that are attached to the bones. They exist for the purpose of allowing us to move the various parts of our bodies in the myriad directions that daily life demands. They raise our arms, move our jaws, waggle our fingers, and make it possible to run, walk, sit, lie down, and to make love.

Conscious bodily movements begin in the brain and are initiated by the transmission of nerve impulses. Muscle fibers contract when stimulated and relax when the stimulation ends. There are fibers that contract quickly, and fibers that contract more slowly but with greater strength. When the muscles contract, because of the way that they are attached to the bones, they cause our arms, legs, fingers, and toes to move in the direction we want them to go.

So, if we want to pull something toward us with our hands, we contract our biceps. If we want to push something away from us, we contract our triceps. Depending on which finger we want to waggle at someone, we contract various muscles in the forearm. We learn to do all this automatically when we are tiny children, and it's not until we get to biology class that we find out what has been going on.

That's how muscles move. Now, how does muscular movement affect the body? After a muscle is contracted, there is an increased demand for oxygen and other essential elements to replace the energy depletion of the muscle tissue. If you do a certain movement, say, rising on your tiptoes once or twice, you won't notice the difference. But if you do it twenty times, you will begin to feel a burning sensation in your calf. If you walk at a leisurely pace on level ground, you won't notice any difference, but if you run uphill, your legs will begin to burn and you will become short of breath. When that happens, you have irrefutable proof that your body is using up the energy stored in it.

Let's go a little deeper and make the connection between weight training and losing fat.

When a muscle is contracted under stress—for example, when we are trying to pick up something heavy over and over again—the post-contraction demand for oxygen is greater than it would be if we were merely trying to lift a finger. The greater the amount of weight we are trying to move and the greater the number of times we move it, the greater the amount of effort required to make the contractions. The greater the amount of effort exerted, the greater the subsequent demand for oxygen. The greater the demand, the more the heart and lungs have to work, and the greater the amount of energy used up by the body. Hence, the general conditioning of the body that occurs through systematic weight training.

But there is more. Muscles very quickly become accustomed to a given amount of work. If you increase the number of times you lift a given weight, you will do either one or both of two things: you will tear down tissue and/or you will "pump" or flush the muscle full of blood. Either way, your circulation will get into high gear in the region that is being worked. If you are really out of shape, and if you do a lot of repetitions with as much weight as you can handle, you will feel light-headed in a very short while. The extent of the feeling of lightheadedness is an indication of how out of shape you are. This is because the blood is rushing to the muscles and away from the brain. You should not overdo weightlifting at first, even though the temptation is there. As you get into shape, you will be able to do more work than you would have imagined possible.

By lifting weights progressively—and by that, I mean doing a certain number of reps (repetitions) with a given amount of weight, then increasing the number of reps when you become stronger—you will gain in strength, stamina, and endurance. You will quickly reach a point at which you will be able to add more weight and return to the number of reps you started with. (We will go into more detail about this method in Chapter Four on the exercises.)

A faster and more thorough "pump" of the muscles can be achieved by what is called the "set system." Joe Weider of the Weider barbell company was one of the pioneers of this system of weight training during the 1940s and 1950s. In this system, you do a given number of reps, rest for a minute or two, then do another "set" of reps. Again, if you are a male and training for strength and/or size, you will work with maximum poundages, pushing to the limit each time, and increasing sets, reps, and/or weight whenever possible. On the other hand, if you are female and your primary aim is to shape your body by peeling the fat away and toning up the muscles, you would not attempt record poundages but instead would concentrate on "burning" the particular muscle being exercised with light weights and multiple sets, so as to flush the blood through the circulatory system that feeds the muscle. At the same time, you would be utilizing the stored fat in that area in particular and stored fat throughout the body in general.

For that's the secret, you see. If you have a lot of energy stored in the form of fat, and if you are burning up more calories in the weightlifting movements than you are taking in in the form of food, you will easily deplete the fat supply. You have to metabolize your stored energy, you have to literally *burn it up*, but it will go if you use it up through exercise. This follows the basic laws of thermodynamics, and they haven't been repealed yet, even by the 30-minute-a-week fitness people, although those hucksters would like to convince you otherwise.

In plain language, what we are saying is this: there is no

more effective way to burn off body fat than through weight training, and the reason that this is true lies in the very laws that govern the biochemistry of your body. Energy is required for work. When you work, you deplete your stocks of energy. Use up more energy than you are taking in and you tap into the energy that is stored in the form of fat.

Obviously, if you continue to eat food rich in carbohydrates and high in calories (thus storing energy in excess of your energy demands), all the working out in the world will not make you lose fat. But if you combine a reduction of carbohydrates and calories with a thorough, concentrated workout of your muscles, the fat will go away.

Take a look at the boys in the muscle magagines. Get a copy of *Iron Man*, *Strength and Health*, *Muscle*, or *Muscular Development*. Forget for a moment that such exaggeration of male musculature might be repulsive to you, and think instead about what these men have been able to do with their fatty tissue. You may not agree with their conception of male beauty, but you will have to admit that they sure don't have any fat on them. Dave Draper, a former Mr. Universe, was the high school fat boy. By judicious dieting and progressive weight training, Draper became famous for the rock-hard definition that characterizes his physique.

We can approach this in a slightly different way.

Why do you want to lose weight? Usually, the answer is, "I'm fat and I want to be slim." But being slim and weighing less are not necessarily the same thing. To be sure, if you weighed 200 pounds and trained down to 125 pounds, you would be noticeably slimmer. But just losing weight is not necessarily what you may want to do. Muscle weighs more per cubic inch than fat. If you are only a few pounds "overweight" and you tone up your muscles, you may not lose much weight at all, but you will redistribute the weight that you have. Also, you can eventually reach a point in weight training where you will not lose any more weight and may even put on a couple of pounds, especially if you have previously debilitated yourself through bad diets in which you have lost significant muscle tissue along with the fat.

Your doctor may smile knowingly and tell you that you "can't lose weight segmentally." Maybe not, but you can sure turn unsightly fat into smooth, shapely, well-contoured muscle segmentally. So you don't lose any weight on your lower leg. So what? You've traded unseemly fat for a shapely calf.

Overall fat will come off from dieting. However, unless you do some sort of exercise while you are dieting, you will have muscle tissue loss too. That's what Dr. Atkins and Dr. Stillman don't tell you. Dr. Linn has the right idea biochemically: you should supplement your diet with some form of predigested protein in order not to suffer muscle tissue loss. Be careful, though. Unless you are grossly overweight, the predigested protein diet can be dangerous. Recent reports of ten women who suffered fatal heart attacks while on the diet should be sufficient warning to make you consult a doctor before going on such a diet. In fact, Linn himself advises against the predigested protein diet unless you are under strict medical supervision. (We'll go a little deeper into the hazards of dieting in Chapter Six.)

What happens if you don't exercise during dieting? Rigorous dieting without exercise will result in loose skin, a pallor that indicates a low energy level, and bulges in problem areas in spite of the weight loss. Anyone who has ever dieted seriously for any length of time knows exactly what I'm talking about. If you are going to have a pleasing shape, you've got to exercise. Diet alone won't do the job.

Weight loss is sometimes a false issue. The important thing, the thing always to keep uppermost in your mind, is that you want to condition your body and get it into the right *shape*. You want to "get in shape" both figuratively and actually. You want to be trim, regardless of what your body type may be. The fact is that you can work muscles more intensely through weight training than through any other form of exercise. You can isolate particular areas of your body, and work specific muscles until the fat around them is jarred into moving. You can work a particular muscle until it just won't contract anymore. No fat deposit will stay on top of a muscle that is being worked that way. Combine a proper diet with weight training and you can't help but lose fat—it's against the laws of thermodynamics not to.

A few sentences back, we mentioned body types. You should know about them, because they are almost always

17

cited in diet and exercise literature. There's nothing difficult about the concept—it's just a common categorization. Anatomists sometimes classify the human body into three types: endomorphs, mesomorphs, and ectomorphs. Most successful high fashion models are true ectomorphs: bony, skinny, tall, and fragile (and many of them who are *not* true ectomorphs starve themselves to meet the demands of the image). Most athletes, whether male or female (except runners), are mesomorphs: medium-boned, muscular, medium height and weight, neither fat nor skinny. Endomorphs tend to be big-boned, large, and fleshy. If you are a mesomorph, you can't become an ectomorph through diet and exercise. However, you can sure trim yourself down.

Think for a moment about the beautiful mesomorphs you have seen: Brigitte Bardot, the young Elizabeth Taylor, Carol Lynley, Karen Black, Margaux Hemingway, Judy Collins, Olga Korbut, Anna Pavlova, Marlo Thomas, Luciana Pignatelli, Nadia Comenici, Joan Baez, Sophia Loren, Julie Christie, Marilyn Monroe, and 99 percent of the gatefold girls in *Playboy*, *Penthouse*, *Mayfair*, and *Oui*. Even television's darling, Farrah Fawcett-Majors, is not a true ectomorph, as a look at her college photos will reveal.

Although you may appear to be an endomorph, you may be mistaken. You may be a sloppy mesomorph who has let herself go to fat. Whatever you do, don't get caught in the trap of labels. No matter what you are, there are things that can be done, and nothing will help you as much as weight training—witness the incredible self-improvement stories that have dotted the pages of the muscle magazines since their inception forty-six years ago.

The point is this: beauty is not a function of body type. It is a function of overall muscular symmetry and being in trim condition. Why should you want to change your body type? You just want to make the most of the one you have. Each body type has its own potential for development.

Few people fall precisely into any specific body type. Moreover, few people have perfect diets or perfect habits. Few people go through their lives without overindulging sometimes in food, alcohol, laziness, and lethargy. There are so many variables in the development of a human being, and with as many dead ends into which we can trap ourselves, it is foolish to hang labels on ourselves. But all of us have the potential that goes with our particular body type. You can realize that potential through systematic exercise, reasonable diet, and enough rest to build yourself into fitness. You won't change your body type, but you will become the best, shapeliest example of the type that you have. Nothing will help you to realize your full physical potential in shaping your body toward an ideal form faster and more effectively than weight training. If there were a better way, the bodybuilders would have found it long ago.

As for those bodybuilders, if there is resistance to weight training among women, a lot of it revolves around what many women feel to be the utter grotesqueness of all those hypertrophied muscles. The ancient Greeks thought the muscled male form was aesthetically pleasing, and so have sculptors through the ages, but twentieth-century people tend to look only at the female form for physical beauty.

If you take an unbiased look at the champion bodybuilders, however, they resemble Greek statuary. Some men in the sport make specific references to this fact. Whether or not they cite Greek statuary, they all have an ideal toward which they are striving: their primary aim is to shape their bodies into the form that is accepted by the bodybuilding world as the ideal male form. That means a tiny waist, broad shoulders, and legs like oak stumps, all with granite-chiseled definition between the individual muscle groups. Some men become Herculean (John Grimek, Arnold Schwarzenegger, Sergio Oliva and Louie Ferrigno), while others strive for the kind of lean, finely carved symmetry made famous by Steve Reeves, Frank Zane, Vince Gironda, Steve Davis, or Chris Dickerson. The current trend among bodybuilders is toward a lighter build, with more definition and more emphasis on symmetry and less on sheer massiveness and bulk.

Most women we've talked to over the last thirty years react to supersized bodybuilders the same way they react to outlaw motorcycle gangs, snails in the bathtub, roaches in the pantry, sweaty undershirts, and disfiguring diseases. Whether you think bodybuilders are handsome or grotesque, dedicated or just plain nuts, you do have one important thing in common with them: you want a body that has a shape you hold to be ideal. This usually means a body that has a different shape from the one your body presently has.

Your notion of the ideal form may be different from that of the bodybuilders (good thing, since neither your genes nor your hormones will allow you to bulge the way they do), but you do have an ideal and you want to attain it. So, whether or not you approve of the way they look, you can use the same bodysculpturing, shape-changing techniques they use to achieve the results that you want. You will notice the difference within a month. You will see a drastic change within two months. You won't believe it's you in four months.

Why haven't more people caught on to this before? There are good reasons, for women in particular and the public in general. Some can be found in the pressures of popular culture and some in the actions and opinions of incompetent athletic coaches in primary and secondary schools, while other reasons can be found in the ignorance and prejudices of the medical profession. We mentioned in the Introduction the myths that have kept women away from weight training. These myths have sprung up from the culture around us. Dr. Ray Browne, director of the Institute for the Study of Popular Culture and founder of the Popular Culture Association, has been a pioneer in calling our attention to the fact that many of the things that influence us in our day-to-day ideas and actions are a product of the acceptance of popular prejudices and merchandised ideologies. Why don't women exercise with weights? What are the popular notions, the conceptions that we hear every day? The list is easy to compile, and it follows the myths mentioned earlier:

1. "It'll make you grow huge muscles." (Wrong. Wrong genes.)
2. "It's something that only men can do." (Nonsense.)
3. "It's just not feminine." (It's not feminine to be strong, healthy, agile, and slender?)
4. "People will make fun of me." (When you're slim and they're still fat, you get the last laugh.)
5. "I've never heard of such a thing." (Well, now you have.)

What about the athletic coaches, those people who tell girls that they shouldn't do "heavy" exercise because it would cause them to (a) develop "female trouble," (b) grow up to look like freaks, (c) become flat-chested, (d) develop cancer, (e) become sterile, (f) smell like football players? Think about it for a moment. If they taught in grade school, those coaches probably had a bachelor's degree with a major in physical education. Some of them (high school coaches) went on to graduate school, and got an M.A. or an M.S. in education, with a specialization in physical education. We don't mean to put them down, but Valerie was in the academic world for eleven years and was associate dean at a college; Ralph was in the academic world for seventeen years, was the dean of a college of arts and sciences for the last six, and even taught Karate as a hobby at the University of North Dakota. We have met literally hundreds of education professors, dozens of physical education instructors, and thousands of education majors. We are sad to report to you that many professional educators have the same popular prejudices against weight training for women as the general public.

The reasons are simple. Unless the university or college from which the coaches get their training is large and progressive enough to support a full-service gymnasium, women physical education majors have little contact with weight training or bodybuilding. Even at the large schools, weight training is rarely taken seriously by or for women, either faculty or students. There is little or no probability that a female student would come into contact with weight training and bodybuilding directly, or with the people who are interested in that sort of thing, unless she happens to date a man who is into the sport. The result is perpetuation of the myth that women and weights don't mix, with women missing out on the benefit of what bodybuilders have known for the last forty years.

There is more to it than this, however. It has to do with the way the school's athletics budget is sliced. Men's athletics always has a bigger budget than women's athletics, with the big money going to spectator sports for men, such as football, hockey, baseball, basketball, or track and field. That's where the money is, has been, and will continue to be, as long as vice-presidents for university development see team athletics as a means for raising funds from alumni and other donors.

Consequently, equipment for the weightlifting room is pretty far down on the list of priorities. Unless the bodybuilding program is tied in with the football team or with the medical school's rehabilitation or physical therapy courses, or unless there is some enlightened person in the department who already knows about the benefits of weight training and who also has a friend on the budget committee, weights and weight training equipment don't get a large allocation.

The latest way to slip money through the back door for weight training equipment is to ask for exercise machines. (See, it isn't really lifting weights, it's an exercise *machine*.) The machines are major budget items (Arthur Jones' Nautilus machines cost over $35,000 for a basic line), and can thus be more easily justified "in terms of the total program" than could a few thousand dollars for some bars and plates. It doesn't make much sense economically, but then there are a lot of things in the realm of higher education that don't make sense.

The result is that your fledgling female physical education major is usually not educated about the benefits of weight training for women and, as a consequence, neither are you. Whether the cause is budgets, priorities, social pressure, conformity to popular culture, or just plain stupidity, most women who become physical education instructors are pretty well channeled into team sports for girls.

As for the medical profession, it seems natural that doctors of all people would be the ones to consult about what the body can do and can't do, what people who want to shape their bodies should and should not do. After all, prevailing opinion (read "popular prejudice") tells us that nobody knows more about our physical well-being than the physicians who make up that vast group called the "medical profession." To a large extent, this is true. It is not true, however, that medical doctors necessarily know a great deal about the beneficial effects of progressive exercise on the normal, healthy body.

Medically, weight training for women falls roughly in the area of rehabilitation, with relevant input from therapeutic dieticians if you are trying to get rid of fat at the same time that you are trying to become stronger. If you are trying to condition your body and sculpt it into the shape that you want, then you are on a rehabilitation program. Don't expect your gynecologist, dermatologist, pediatrician, or proctologist to be able to say anything particularly edifying about the benefits of weight training as a rehabilitation technique. Unless the particular doctor has specific training in this area, he is probably no more knowledgeable about it than the average well-informed, well-educated person in the street.

Of course, you should see your doctor before launching into a strenuous exercise routine. There is always the possibility that you have a heart condition, high blood pressure, diabetes, dietary deficiencies, or a host of other ailments that might be aggravated by strenuous exercise. Before beginning *any* radical departure from a sedentary lifestyle, you should get a complete physical. The whole idea here is to be healthy, happy, strong, and beautiful. Keep your conscience clear and put your mind at ease. See your doctor and find out if there is anything wrong in your doing strenuous exercise. If you want to hear from the medical profession about the beneficial effects of progressive exercise, however, seek the advice of a professional in the field of athletic medicine or rehabilitation. They're the experts in this particular area, and they will tell you whether you're on the right track.

Let's try to sum it all up in a few sentences before we go on to Valerie's story. Here are the basics:

If you want to trim down, get rid of your fat, regain the natural contours of your body, and generally condition yourself, use light weights, do high repetitions with multiple sets, and eat small amounts of a balanced diet that is restricted in fats, starches, and carbohydrates.

Since you are a woman and have a woman's genes and hormones, instead of building big muscles, your muscles will remain essentially the same size, increase in density and strength, and use the stored energy in your fatty tissue for the work that is done in weight training.

By concentrating your effort on specific body areas, you can burn off fat through weight training, thus sculpting your body into the shape you want.

You can expect results almost immediately, depending on

how fat you are, how out of shape you are, and how serious you are about wanting to make progress. You'll look terrific, feel terrific, and if Valerie is any guide to what you can accomplish, you'll *be* terrific.

CHAPTER 2

Fighting the Fat Demon (Valerie's Story)

"There are Thin Souls and there are Fat Souls."

"Fat children make fat adults."

"You can't change your body type."

"Your fat cells are already and irrevocably developed by age six."

You must know all these familiar homilies backwards and forwards by now. They're part of our current Fat Mythology. They glare at you from the cover of every magazine. They bombard your ears on the way to work every morning. We are living in a culture where Thin is In and Fat is Out.

Because I had been fat all my life, I discovered the other side of the Fat/Thin business almost too late. But I learned, to my great delight, that all those "myths" are true. Thin women *do* have more fun than fat ones. Thin people *are* better treated in stores, restaurants, garages, and airports. Thin people *do* have more energy than fat ones. Junior clothes *do* cost less than Chubby Misses sizes. And Thin is not just better-looking—it is also healthier than Fat.

In my previous incarnation as a Fat Soul, I was never any competition for Mama Cass. But I was Fat. I had plump arms, a round little protruding tummy, a veritable shelf of a *derrière*, bulging thighs, and piano legs with thick ankles. What's more, I had them from age twelve until the magic day in 1973 when I hauled out the weights and started on the Bodysculpture routine that finally led to the New Me.

My peak weight was about 175 pounds. But more typically, it was 155 to 160—heavy for a 5'6" frame but not impossible. But my "thin" times were more a curse than a blessing. They delivered only false hopes. I could easily drop down to 145 or 150 without making an inch's difference in my measurements. I never got quite bad enough to pack myself off to a fat farm, spa, or hospital for help with my "problem." I always thought that tomorrow would bring a solution. Tomorrow I would magically wake up thin. So I dragged along for fifteen years, yo-yo-ing between thin phases and fat phases.

I was a cuddly baby, an adorably chubby toddler, a plump little girl, a chunky pre-teen, a stocky adolescent, and finally a self-loathing graduate student who starved herself down to 135 pounds on a balanced diet of black coffee and No-Doz. One year, one marriage, and one Ph.D. dissertation later, I ballooned back up to 175.

My perpetual weight problem was not the result of laziness, negligence about diet, or some other error of my misspent youth. Far from it. From age twelve on, I was literally obsessed with being thin. I sighed over the slenderness of fictional heroines like Anne of Green Gables (described as a skinny but potentially elegant adolescent), Daphne Du Maurier's ghostly Rebecca, Dumas' wraithlike Camille. Inspired by these literary archetypes, I embarked on an austere diet which horrified my mother and grandmother. One egg, one small salad, one scoop of cottage cheese, and one hamburger patty per day was it. In addition to mortifying the flesh with diet, I also rolled on the floor, bumped, ground, skipped rope, walked, and ran. Finally, in the last stages of my madness, I clipped exercises from the *Ladies' Home Journal* which I performed like a demented whirling dervish in pitch darkness on my bedroom rug at night.

After an initial loss of three pounds, nothing happened. The scales and tape measure stayed just where they were, and I settled in for an almost lifelong battle with the Fat Demon.

Constant childhood bouts with pneumonia and a chronic middle ear infection had kept me from learning to swim, water ski, or play basketball. I was too ashamed of my legs to wear shorts, so I got excused from gym on the pretext of "allergies." I heard that acrobatics and tap dancing were good for fat legs and immediately enrolled in dancing class. I was thrown out in ten days by a disgruntled teacher who told me that my legs were disgusting, and that I could never be a "daffodil" in the Junior High Follies Night, let alone a ballerina.

So I kept score at volleyball games, never bought a bathing suit, skipped town during the class picnic, and affected sneers for short shorts, Bermudas, and toreador pants. Actually I was wild with envy. The fifties and sixties of *American Graffiti* were something the other kids did. I bundled up in heavy coats during the winter. During the summers I mostly hid.

Another bout with an inner ear infection sent me down to 125 pounds the summer before college. True, I still had my piano legs and the rear end that wouldn't quit, but I also acquired a waist, reasonably thin arms, and a fashionably gaunt face. *Now* I was getting somewhere. I did the sensible thing. I visited my friendly family physician and asked his advice. I did not want to regain the lost weight, and I also wanted to "do something" about my legs and hips. I was tired of looking dumpy. I wanted to have pretty legs, wear short skirts, a bikini even. It didn't seem too much to ask.

The good doctor weighed me, consulted the height-weight chart on the wall, told me that I was, if anything, a little underweight for my height, prescribed some vitamin pills, and told me not to worry. My legs were "just fine" for my height (never mind that I couldn't find a pair of slacks to fit over my thighs). My heavy ankles were "genetic" and were just a part of my lot in life, to be borne with fortitude and grace. I was a fine, healthy girl and it was "neurotic" to be so obsessed with weight problems. Pressed for further advice, he suggested that I consult a shrink about my desire to be thin.

College and graduate school days were a classic case of the yo-yo syndrome. If I ate normally, I tipped the scales at 135–140; if I starved myself, I could force that devilish little needle down to 130. Once, after an attack of pneumonia, I got all the way down to 124. But did my legs respond? No, quite the contrary: I had a gaunt face with hollow cheekbones that would have done credit to Camille, a pair of skeletal arms, bony shoulders, and a 32-inch bust topping the familiar piano legs and bulging ankles. I wept and consoled myself with another scoop of cottage cheese.

It was during this period of my life that I learned about two kinds of doctors. The first type was always aghast at my bulges: "Good God, you're overweight! Take these red pills, six after each meal, eat nothing but grapefruit and cottage cheese, and come back next Tuesday . . ." The second type, usually inclined to fat himself, was more sanguine. His stock-in-trade was complacence tempered by benign neglect: "You women are all alike, all wanting legs like Bardot's. You're healthy and sturdy, nothing wrong with you. Just genetics is all. Heavy ankles run in your family? I thought so. Nothing you can do about that. Relax and forget about it."

Several doctors prescribed psychotherapy. Others prescribed diet pills, which made me kick the cat, the walls, and anything else within easy reach. One did an elaborate and expensive series of tests which confirmed his original diagnosis: there was nothing wrong with me except excessive vanity, galloping neurosis, and an obsession with thin legs. Even the best of the lot said, "You can't lose weight segmentally: you can't cheat nature," and laughed at my attempts to exercise the fat away.

Luckily for me, I met Ralph during a winter when dark stockings, overblouse sweaters, and ski pants with boots were fashionable, so his memory of the lower part of my anatomy was reasonably vague when he proposed marriage. A year later, I moved my stash of diet cookbooks, jump ropes, and exercise clippings into our new apartment and determined to turn myself into a raving beauty for this most deserving of husbands. But a combination of the Pill, my new delight in gourmet cooking (he ate while I absorbed calories through osmosis), and late-night fast-food snacks added 20 pounds. A *thin* Ph.D. I was not.

Ironically, it was the wonderful world of Mod fashion that set me on the right track. I went out to buy wedding clothes and found nothing that I could cram my beefy thighs into except a matronly white suit. The stores were filled with racks and racks of wonderful things: skinny velveteen flowered bell-bottoms with poor-boy sweaters, Pucci-printed dresses, bare midriff blouses, and miniskirts, miniskirts, miniskirts. Ralph loved the new styles and so did I. But not one of them came in a size 16. I went home and cried myself to sleep—a fat, matronly, dumpy little bride.

The trousseau fiasco sent me on the diet of all diets: two hardboiled eggs per day, one scoop of cottage cheese, and one small salad with oil and vinegar, supplemented by gargantuan portions of Tab, plain soda water, and black coffee. Slowly the pounds came off, although the inches stayed on. Still, by fall I was able to buy a gray pinstripe miniskirt with a chain belt. I wore it with heavy black opaque tights and hoped that no one noticed my 12-inch ankles.

Ralph, bless him, was touched by my struggles with the Fat Demon. He had been a childhood victim of rheumatic fever and had weightlifted his way back to health. He was back into weights again and suggested that I try it too. Alas, I was so weak by this time from the constant dieting and so totally unathletic as a result of my nonswimming, nonrunning, nondancing adolescence that I could barely lift one leg off the floor and hold it to a count of five.

Slowly, however, we began to work out an exercise routine for me. I did it spasmodically because I felt so listless and debilitated from the diet. And I used no weights at all because, like most women, I had grown up hostile to weightlifting. I didn't want big muscles, I protested. I didn't want to be strong. I just wanted to look like Twiggy and Veruschka and all those other marvelously lanky, long-legged models who skipped through every page of *Vogue* and *Bazaar*.

I did have one brief period of success, which should have taught me a lesson but didn't. Like most American women I was too prejudiced against bodybuilding to pay attention. The university where I taught had a large "Universal Gym" machine. I watched with mounting curiosity on weekends when Ralph taught his Karate class and then migrated to the weights room for a short session. At his suggestion, I worked out with light weights on a very simple routine of exercises for about six weeks. I noticed that my legs were beginning to take on a better contour, that I lost inches and tired less easily. That should have convinced me of the value of weight training. But along came a new job, promotions for us both, and exercise was lost in the excitement of the big move to Chicago.

I started my new job weighing about 135, still with my heavy legs and hips. I worked out for the first summer with a ballet and modern dance class, and then forgot *them* as the pressures of the new job began to take hold. Karate classes and the university gym had kept me going previously, but now I did nothing. I ballooned back to 155 pounds and acquired a protruding tummy, a hipline that measured 47 inches, and a definite spare tire around the middle.

During this unhappy period, I stumbled across a copy of Luciana Pignatelli's *The Beautiful People's Beauty Book*. I agonized over all the pictures of sleek jet-setters with their taut muscles, trim waists, and lean legs. Some of the photos in the book astonished me—they showed the incredibly svelte Luciana in leotard and ankle weights, exercising and pounding her cellulite away. I was immensely encouraged. If this suntanned darling of the Idle Rich would do *weightlifting*, then so would I. I remembered my brief success with the Universal Gym in North Dakota. Now I had no exercise machine to use. Chicago's health clubs were prohibitively expensive and the university gym offered only a broken stationary bicycle and a few rusty bars and plates. But we still had our own Sears plates, several sets of handles and collars, and a pair of iron boots. I invested in a pair of 3-pound ankle weights and a pair of 2½-pound "Smart Belles" for bust and arm exercises.

In contrast to my six-week blitz in North Dakota, this time

Midway through Bodysculpture .

I took it all slowly. I didn't drop my food intake so dangerously low. I reduced my carbohydrate intake, and I cut out all breads, pastries, pastas, cereals, and syrup-packed fruits. But I continued to eat eggs, yogurt, berries, melon, chicken, fish, lean beef, salads, and raw vegetables for snacks. Lots of fresh-squeezed vegetable juice (unsalted), unsweetened grapefruit juice, and mineral water were part of my daily diet. I also ate a little wheat germ and raw honey for energy, or dropped a spoonful of honey into lemon tea for a midafternoon snack. I took a multivitamin pill and several high-protein tablets a day. But the major difference between this routine and the dozens of regimens from the past was a big one. Now, with Ralph's help, I began serious weight training. Between the two of us, we discovered Bodysculpture, the feminine version of bodybuilding. And I learned that I could, at last, have the body I'd always wanted.

I had had a long layoff, so I had to take it slowly at first. I was weak, out of shape, and had no stamina. The new diet was so different from my old sloppy eating habits that I had trouble adjusting. I was tired all the time—too tired even to support the ankle weights or lift the Smart Belles. But I came home three nights a week and went through a general routine of conditioning exercises (see our "Beginner's Module") which I did without weights at first, just to get the movements right and get myself started.

I also did some stretching exercises to help loosen up my tight muscles (see the Karate stretching exercises in the exercises section—I still use them for limbering and relaxing). After two months, I had long since added weights in all the exercises. By August, only four and a half months after I started, I had lost 3 inches from my waist, 3 from each thigh,

And now

2 from each calf, and most spectacular of all, my hips had shrunk from 47 to 38 inches. In May, I had combed the stores for just one pair of jeans that would fit me. Now I walked out of chic stores in tight French jeans. By September, Ralph photographed me in a new size 10 bikini—my first real bathing suit. We both had to look twice at the photo to believe that this was the girl who had fought the Fat Demon all her life.

I continued the workout routine with light weights into the fall and winter that year. Ralph was also seriously back into bodybuilding for the first time in more than twenty years. The His and Her workout sessions on weekends were a great incentive to us both. We invested in a small workout bench for the study at home and built a slant board from 2×4's padded with a blanket. By spring, thanks to the situps and leg raises, my waist was down to 26 inches and my hips to 36. The original French jeans were now too large for me, and I had to settle for an American copy from a *junior* department. Ditto for all my clothes: I discovered smaller-than-small departments and 5-7-9 shops for the first time.

Thus far my workout routine had been quite general—after all, there was so much to lose. I had concentrated on the big (and embarrassing) trouble spots: waist, midriff, hips. Now I was beginning to look positively thin everywhere except in my legs. So I started a specialized leg routine, using precisely the exercises recommended by leading bodybuilders. By now we had realized the basic principle of Bodysculpture: that women respond to bodybuilding in a different way than men. I did the so-called Big Five for legs: leg curls, leg extensions, rises on toes, half squats, and leg presses (we will explain them in detail later). The results were amazing. I soon discovered two kneecaps, assorted muscular patterns in my thighs, and best of all, two ankle bones. My thighs hollowed out and my calves developed definite contours. Not quite Camille, but definitely not a Fat Soul either.

Later that year, I added running to my routine. I started slowly, at a quarter-mile a day, and worked up to a mile a day. Again, the results were spectacular. After two months, I dropped an inch from my waist, two inches from my hips, another inch from my thighs, and an inch from my calves.

CHAPTER 3

Psyching Up: The Right Mental Attitude for Maximum Success

So far, we've done a lot of talking about your body. Before we go on to the exercise program, let's talk a little bit about your mind. As you probably already know, it is next to impossible to get the most out of anything you attempt if you don't have the right mental attitude. Exercising is no different from any other endeavor in this respect.

Let's use Ralph's own experience to illustrate the point. For some time before his 40th birthday, he had been thinking about resuming an exercise routine. He had begun to look in the mirror every day, grimace at what he saw, and quickly put on a coat to hide the fat that was building up around his waist. Further, since he had had rheumatic fever when he was a child, he knew full well the dangers of becoming fat and out of shape. The pressures of a new job, writing a book, and moving to a new city had taken their toll. He was trying to build himself up to the point where he would make a commitment to getting back in shape, but he wasn't quite there yet.

A series of events pushed him over the edge to decision. He

couldn't get into last year's suit, he got out of breath when the elevator broke down and he had to climb two flights of stairs. At lunch he realized that he had eaten 13 patties of butter and all the rolls in the basket, and he almost fell asleep at his desk during the afternoon.

The last straw came on the way home. He worked seven blocks from our apartment. Halfway home, he was out of breath again, and he realized something that had been nagging at his mind all along: he walked like an old man. His belly sagged, his feet pointed outward, and he had none of the grace that he had developed years before when he taught Karate. He was completely out of shape, and his body no longer moved in the way he wanted it to move. It moved in the way that it *had* to move, given a redistribution of body fat and his woeful condition.

When he got home, he took his usual shower and automatically headed for the refrigerator. He stopped for a moment and remembered what he had realized on the way home.

It took another couple of days for him to admit to himself that he simply *had* to do something. He dragged out his barbell plates that he had saved all those years, and tried to go through a workout. It was laughable. He could barely work with 60 pounds (now he uses 350). But he persisted, and went through the rest of the workout. He was sore the following day, but past experience told him that the soreness meant progress. With only a few exceptions, he has been on a regular workout routine ever since, and that has been six years now.

What Ralph had done was to get his mind made up to make his body do what it needed to do. In practical terms, we tend to think of our bodies and minds as separate things. Actually, our minds and bodies are simply two aspects of the same thing: ourselves. It's not that the body works for the mind. The mind *and* the body work for *you*, to accomplish what *you* want to do.

The point is simple: the proper mental attitude is of utmost importance in Bodysculpture; the right attitude will greatly enhance your ability to achieve your physical goals. This is true whether we are talking about your attitude in general or your particular mental set during a particular workout. It comes in stages. First you have to make your mind up. Then you have to make your body do what the mind tells it to do. Then you have to sustain the mental commitment to go on and accomplish the goals that you have set for yourself. In Ralph's case, as he realized walking home from work that day, he had become ashamed of his body. He had also become ashamed of his mind, for lacking the resolve that it takes to pull out of the middle-aged trap he had gotten himself into. First, he literally had to *make up his mind*. Then he had to make his body obey his mind. Then he had to keep going, in spite of his body's soreness and his mind's desire to become lazy.

To put it in plain language, nobody can lose that fat and sculpt your body but *you*. There's no use in kidding yourself. You've got to put your foot down, once and for all, and give yourself some orders. Then you've got to follow those orders. If you do, then you'll succeed. If you don't, you won't. It's as simple as that. The self-help sections of every bookstore are full of magazines, pamphlets, and books that shout out at you in Day-glo colors about magical and effortless ways to lose weight and get in shape. Everybody would like to be able to reshape himself or herself with no effort. The people who write those books know that, and that's why they tell you that you don't have to put out any effort to lose weight, get in condition, gain mystical insights, and all the other marvelous things that they promise. Why do they make such promises? To sell books by telling the readers what they would like to hear, that's why.

You've probably already tried some of the routines that such publications recommend. And you probably are discouraged by your lack of progress. Of course you aren't making the progress you want to make. To make the kind of progress you want requires both mental commitment and hard work. But it doesn't have to be drudgery. You'll discover, perhaps to your surprise, that there are few things in the world more gratifying or more exhilarating than the feeling you get when you really push yourself during a workout. Don't take our word for it. Try it for yourself. Then you'll see that the 15-minute-a-week people missed the whole point.

Let us also hasten to say that there is nothing mysterious

about developing the right mental attitude. Modern biofeed-back techniques have demonstrated that you don't have to be from the mountains of Tibet to be able to control your pulse, breathing, and blood pressure. Almost any ordinary person can do it to a certain extent, even though the psychologists can't quite figure out how it works. Many scientists refuse to take biofeedback seriously, although the effects seem clear enough. It is intriguing that anyone should think there is any-thing new about all of this. Athletic coaches in Karate, Judo, Aikido, and other martial arts have known for ages (literally hundreds of years) that truly incredible feats are possible with the right kind of mental discipline. Conversely, they have also known for ages that without the right kind of mental disci-pline, you won't be able to do as well as possible, no matter what you are trying to do.

To clarify things, there are two basic kinds of psyching up that have to be done in order to succeed.

1. You have to make up your mind that you have certain goals, and that you are absolutely and irrevocably determined to reach those goals.
2. You have to go into *each workout* with your mind attuned to making progress toward those goals during that workout.

It's like the old story of the man who "loved humanity" but couldn't stand individual persons. It doesn't do much good to think something generally unless you are able to apply it to the specific case (in this case, to the actual workout).

Since everybody is different from everybody else, there is no single method for psyching up that works for every occa-sion and for everybody. There are some general rules, how-ever, which will help you to get yourself into the right frame of mind to make the most of each workout. Let us go over some of the ones that have worked for us, and are well known by others in the field.

First, it helps to separate your workout from the rest of your daily routine. All those people who advise you to flex your abdominal muscles every day on the way to the water cooler don't know what they are talking about. You need to make the workout important. It needs to be something special.

After all, it's going to change everything for the better, isn't it?

A workout is not merely a matter of going into the kitchen or the basement or the spare bedroom and flailing your arms and legs around for a few minutes. It is not merely working up a sweat while the hi-fi belts out the latest reggae record. Let us take a big chance, a chance that you will take us seriously when we say it: a workout is something almost *sacred*. It is something unique, something that belongs to you and you alone. It is *your* mind that is being disciplined. It is *your* body that is being shaped. It is *your* muscles that get sore. It is the communion of *your* mind with *your* body. It is a joyous journey into *your* self.

Make the workout something special. Make it a work of art, with a beginning, a middle, and an end. Make it a time when you can be perfectly and completely honest with yourself. Don't worry about feeling embarrassed if at first it seems silly to be so serious about all this, but it is necessary that you understand what working out is really all about.

Forget everything that anybody has ever told you about athletes, locker rooms, jocks, dim-witted ballplayers, and the rest of the self-defeating garbage that people hide behind when they haven't the initiative to take the plunge themselves. Also, forget the jocks and ballplayers you knew in high school or college who *were* dim-witted or gross. That's *them*. It has nothing to do with the value of exercise.

Forget the advice of those people who tell you that all you need is a few minutes of belly-flexing a day while sweeping the floor to the sounds of disco rock. They're like the orgasm experts who've never had one. With their attitude, how could they possibly know the joy of really communing with their bodies?

When you are going into a workout, go *into* the workout. Make the trip. If you go into it in this way, then you will make progress ten times faster, because you won't be fighting yourself and the world around you. You will be fighting the real enemy, with all the concentration and skill and focus possible. You will be fighting the Fat Demon.

Okay, that's the right general attitude. How about psyching

up for the actual workout? Different things work for different people. Here are a few things that work for us.

Each morning, Valerie does the Yoga Sun Greeting. Since she is a "morning" person anyway, she does most of her exercises quite early. After she finishes watering the plants, she stands before the window, hands in front as if in prayer, and breathes deeply as she raises her hands above her head, as far back as possible. Then, she bends and touches her toes, her hands still together. The rest of the Yoga Sun Greeting goes as follows:

After touching your toes, assume a partially kneeling position, with the left leg bent up to the chest and the right leg back. Then stretch both legs out together, supporting your weight on your toes. Lower your body down and rest your forehead on the floor. Hold the position for several seconds, then breathe in and push your body up by straightening your arms. Then bring the hips up as far as possible. Assume a partially kneeling posture again, this time reversing the leg positions (right leg to chest, left one to the back). Repeat the first three motions in reverse order (touch your fingertips to the floor, breathe deeply while straightening up and reaching back, then return the hands to the prayer position).

Valerie then follows the Sun Greeting by sitting on the floor for a few moments in the classic Yoga posture, with the legs crossed and the feet interlocked. To finish the posture properly, you should hold your hands loosely on the knees, with the thumbs and forefingers forming an "O." With your eyes closed, meditate for a few moments before your workout.

Ralph uses a totally different routine. It is the ritual used by the Japan Karate Association *Senseis* (instructors) before each workout. It is a perfect example of how to develop the kind of mental and physical discipline necessary in making the workouts special occasions for you. Remember: the important thing here is getting psyched up to do what is necessary to accomplish your goals. Your goals are to sculpt your body and improve your physical condition—literally, to get in shape and get into the right shape.

At the beginning of every Karate workout, when the *Karatekas* (persons who follow the "Way of Karate") come into the *dojo* (workout room), they bow. This bow is to the *dojo* itself, to the arena, to all the *Karatekas* who have worked out there in the past and who will work out there in the future. It is a bow of respect to the "field" in which Karate is to be done, for the people who will do Karate in that "field," and, lastly, for the art of Karate itself.

Next, the *Sensei* causes the *Karatekas* to form a line, with the highest-ranking person at one end and the lowest-ranking person at the other, all facing the *Sensei*. They drop to their knees, placing the right big toe over the left big toe, then settle back on the backs of their heels. The *Sensei* looks at the people before him, and at the appropriate time calls out "*Makso* (meditate)!" The people sit with their backs straight, hands on their legs, eyes closed, meditating. Next, the *Sensei* shouts "*Yame* (end meditation)!" and the *Karatekas* open their eyes, thus ending the short meditation. Finally, the *Sensei* calls out "*Re* (bow)!" and the people bow deeply, their palms downward, with their faces touching the backs of their hands as they place their hands on the floor before them. Then, they all jump to their feet as if transformed.

What is this all about? In theory, by undertaking the ritual, everything that happened to you between the last workout and this one is forgotten. Time itself is changed, and the life that is spent outside the *dojo* disappears. The ritual erases the gaps in between workouts, so that life is a continuous workout. The life of the *Karateka* is the life of the *dojo*. There is no other life when he is at the *dojo*. When he is not at the *dojo*, he is living the illusory life, which will be erased by the ritual when he returns to the *dojo*. In a spiritual sense, then, the *Karateka* never leaves the *dojo*. It *is* his life.

In practice, the ritual calls attention to the fact that to be in the *dojo* is something special, something more than merely a group of people working up a sweat in a Karate studio. It pulls the workout out of the ordinary and makes it something special. Insofar as the ritual is successful, all the participants become a part of the "something special" that the *dojo* helps to create.

There is another concept in Karate that further illustrates the point, and which can be used to create the frame of mind that will enable you to be aggressive in pursuing your goals. It is called *Mizu no kokoro*, and means "making the mind like water." If you were staring at a pool of water, and this pool was the only way that you could see the approach of an enemy, it would be essential that the surface of the pool be calm and undisturbed. If there are ripples, you will not be able to interpret correctly the approach of the enemy, and he will kill you. On the other hand, if the pool is calm and undisturbed, then the reflection in it will be clear and you will be able to take whatever steps are necessary to defend yourself.

Consider the mind to be that pool. If the mind is disturbed by fear and self-doubt, you will not be able to see clearly what the enemy is doing or planning. And the enemy will kill you. Thus, the mind must be like the water in the pool.

Mizu no kokoro.

Be calm.

Serene.

Self-possessed.

Nothing mysterious, really, just plain good sense. And what's more, it works.

But who is the enemy? Well, for the *Karateka* it is the opponent, the person who is trying to attack and kill him. But who is the real enemy? The *Sensei* knows the answer, and it is found in the concept of the mind being like a calm pool of water. The real enemy is *yourself*. It is *your* fear that ripples the water, that keeps you from seeing the attacker clearly. It is *your* doubts that will kill you in the end. The attacker is only the instrument of your defeat. Ultimately, you are defeated by yourself.

Once more: nothing mysterious, just good sense. In fact, if it weren't so out of style, it would be called "wisdom." Let's be unstylish for a moment. It *is* wisdom. It is a matter of understanding something important about yourself and about the frame of mind you must have if you are to succeed.

Instant recap:

1. Set aside a certain part of each day. That's *your* time. Keep the others out. If they won't grant you this time for yourself, then take it from them. They have no right to it. It is *yours*.

2. Calm yourself. Do the Karate ritual. Or try Valerie's Yoga Greeting to the Sun. Or just a quiet prayer (don't ever be ashamed to ask for help). Find your own mantra and say it. Pull yourself *out* of the everyday world around you.

3. Close your eyes and feel yourself moving into another dimension. Imagine a place that is one second out of phase with the space-time frame in which you usually live. Let your mind slip into that place. Break on through to the other side.

Now. Do the workout. The exercises that you perform are sacred acts that you do for yourself. They are private, inner experiences that only *you* know and feel. Do each exercise with the same concentration and attention that an artist would give to the brush strokes of a painting or that a musician would give to the strings of his lute.

But never forget that you are also fighting a battle, a battle for your very life. You fight this battle in this *private* way, with concentration and intensity, but it is a battle nevertheless. Cut through everything until you have your goal in sight. You know what it is: you must kill the Fat Demon before he kills you.

Ready? Let's go.

CHAPTER 4

The Exercises: What They Are, How They Work, How to Get the Best Possible Results

Now we get to the heart of it. Let us say a few things about the exercises described in this chapter: what they are, why we've described them the way we have, and how to use this section when you work your exercise routines up from the advice in the chapter that follows.

First, there is no jazzy way to write a description of an exercise or any physical activity. The more elaborate the description, the more difficult it often is to figure out exactly what is being described. The easiest way to understand a particular physical activity is by example, of course.

When Ralph first got into Karate, Mr. Takiyuki Mikami, a chief instructor for the Japan Karate Association, would walk up and down the line of students, looking at them and how they did the movements. When they did things right (rarely) he would smile and give a nod of approval. When they did them wrong, he would reach out and move their arms and legs in the directions that they should be going. When the students persisted in doing things wrong, he would give them a tap (sometimes a whop!) and *make* them do them right. He watched them like a hawk, and was ready to swoop down at any moment to correct their errors. If they had questions, he would answer them with an illustration of the correct movement. It was easy to follow, since there was no language barrier. It was the language of the body, not verbal language. They learned quickly and thoroughly, and the lessons stayed with them.

Here, you are learning not from "body language" but from words. We have to find the right words to make up for the absence of a coach or instructor. Consequently, we've tried to be as brief, clear, and to the point as possible.

If the exercises seem a little dry in their description, it's because we believe that it's better to keep unfamiliar things simple than to obscure them by being overly cute.

Each exercise is accompanied by photographs, so that you can see what is being described as well as hear the description as you read it to yourself. If you follow things carefully, you should have no trouble doing the exercises the right way.

To help you follow the exercise descriptions and to familiarize you with the terminology, here is an outline of what's covered. We've broken the exercises down into specific body areas, with an initial section on limbering and stretching.

THE EXERCISES

BODYSCULPTURE

EXERCISES (CONTINUED)

BODYSCULPTURE

EXERCISES (CONTINUED)

Sounds like a foreign language, doesn't it? Don't worry. What you've just read is simply the traditional names of the traditional exercises. Before you know it, these names will be as familiar as old friends. Don't be discouraged at the newness of it all. The results will be more than worth the small amount of effort expended in learning the terminology of exercising.

You are also probably wondering about the kinds of equipment you will need to do these exercises listed above. Before we go any further, let's talk about the equipment: what it is, what it looks like, what it's made of, where to get it, and how much it costs. Here is a list.

A WORKOUT SUIT

Basic Workout Suit

This can be a leotard, a jogging suit, a Karate or Judo uniform, a sweatsuit, gym shorts and a T-shirt, or anything that you prefer so long as it doesn't restrict your movements. The climate you live in determines part of it. There is no way you can work out in a sweatsuit on the Gulf Coast in July. Valerie prefers a rubberized Weider "Panther" suit, with a front zipper. She uses it because it increases perspiration and helps keep her water retention problem under control. If you don't retain fluids, this may not be a consideration for you. Whatever your preference, you'll want to wear this outfit whenever you work out. It's part of the discipline of the Bodysculpture routine you're trying to establish.

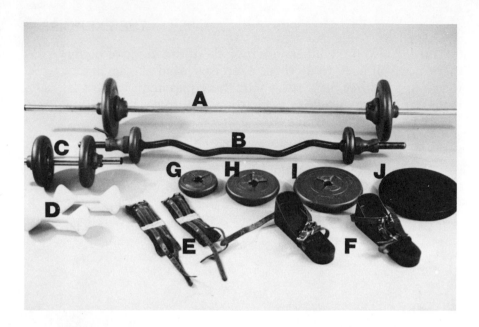

Basic Equipment
A. Barbell
B. Curling Bar
C. Dumbbell
D. "Smart Belles"
E. Ankle Weights

F. Iron boots
G. 2½-pound plate
H. 5-pound plate
I. 10-pound plate
J. 25-pound plate

A BARBELL SET

This is the basic piece of equipment that will help you to shape your body. It consists of a long metal bar, with disc-shaped plates on the ends. You'll use it for twists, good morning exercises, calf raises, squats, curls, presses, and many more of the exercises listed above and described in this chapter. There are many brand names: York, Eleiko, Weider, Healthways, Sears, Jox, and many others. They can be bought at almost any athletic equipment store. If money is no object, there are sets that are completely chrome plated. If you want to hold the costs down, there are economy models everywhere from Sears to the local health food store. Weight is weight, so the fancy chrome isn't necessary unless you want to keep the pieces lying around the living room as *objets d'art*.

On the other hand, you should look closely at the workmanship. Some of the off-brands are really poorly machined. It is better to stick with whatever is being sold by your local reputable athletic store. If you don't know where to go, look in the Yellow Pages. If there is nothing there, then call the local high school or YMCA and ask them where they bought their weights. If you can lay down the cash (or the credit card) go ahead and get a 110-pound set. That way, you'll get the bar, all the collars to hold the weights on with, two dumbbell handles with their own collars, and enough plates to allow you to make the maximum progress up to and beyond your initial program.

DUMBBELLS

These are miniature barbells, to be held in each hand. If you get the 110-pound set, they're included. If you don't buy a set, you'll need dumbbells anyway, for use in some of the special exercises where you are really trying to get right down to the square inch of area to be worked out. They're essential for side leans, and in combination with the iron boots (see the following) if you decide to get a pair of them also.

ANKLE WEIGHTS AND/OR IRON BOOTS

You'll want to get a set of ankle weights, in the 2½-pound or 3-pound weight. They're made of weighted suede, canvas, or leather, and can be strapped around each ankle. Very effective calf and thigh reducers they are, and also good for many abdominal and hip exercises.

A slightly more ambitious version is the iron boots, which are actually metal "sandals" which can be strapped on your feet or over tennis shoes. They weigh about 5 pounds each and are very effective when you do the leg and hip exercises. While the strap-on ankle weights may be good enough to start with, you'll soon graduate to the iron boots, so go ahead and buy them now. They'll be found in most sporting goods stores or in sports equipment sections of department stores.

BARBELL PLATES

These are the discs that fit onto the ends of the barbells and dumbbells. If you get the 110-pound set, you'll have all the plates in all the combinations you'll need. If you don't buy a whole set, you'll need the following: four 10-pound plates, four 5-pounders, and four 2½-pounders. Plates come in all sizes and shapes. Some are cast iron, some are chrome-plated metal, and some are shot-filled vinyl. The last kind are a godsend to the apartment dweller, since they don't make a clanking noise when they strike against each other. Also, they don't mar floors when you set the things down too hard. Again, look for good workmanship. Weightlifting has become so popular, you should have no trouble in finding precisely what you need at a price that is right for you.

When you buy equipment, keep in mind that you can buy all that you need for a 90-day program for less than $65. You can outfit an entire home gym for less than $300 (I mean really heavy equipment for long range serious Bodysculpture), while memberships in the most economical neighborhood gyms start somewhere around $125, and a year's membership in a fancy health spa tops out at around $450 to $500 a year. If you ever want to go all out, you can buy an elaborate multi-purpose home exercise machine made of the finest steel, heavily enameled, with about fifteen exercises possible in a single machine for about $1,000.

All well and good, but what you need to spend is about $65 on basic barbell equipment. That's one of the things that is so great about weight training—it doesn't cost a lot of money if you know what to do and what to buy. That's what this book is for.

Now that we know what equipment to buy, we need to learn the terminology of exercising itself. In this chapter the exercises are divided into preliminary stretching and limbering, then seven sections: Shoulders, Back, Waist, Hips, Thoracic Area, Arms, and Legs. Each section is composed of a number of different exercises for specific parts of the body. For example, the section called "The Waist" is divided into four exercises for the abdominal muscles and four for the sides or external oblique muscles. The section on "The Hips" is divided into "high hips," "middle hips," and "lower hips." Each of the specific exercises is exactly that: an *exercise*, consisting of movements of the body such as leg raises, situps, lunges, or squats.

Combine all the exercises within a given section and you have what we call a *module*. So, there is a waist module, a hip module, a back module, a leg module, and so on. Each of these modules represents what you'll be doing to reshape a particular part of your body. If you combine several modules together and then go do them in a workout, that is your *routine* for that particular workout. If you look at all the exercises in all the modules that you have used in your workout routines, then that constitutes the total *program* that you have devised to solve your problems.

Let's go over it again. It's not really complicated. All we want to do is to agree on terminology, so that we won't have any misunderstandings when we describe the various things that go into your program.

Remember this way of talking about all these things:

1. An *exercise* is a movement that works a muscle or group of muscles in the body.

2. *Reps* are repetitions of a specific exercise movement.

3. A *set* is a specific exercise, done for a given number of reps. For instance, you might do three *sets* of ten *reps* of the squat. That would mean that you did the squat movement ten times, rested for a few minutes, did ten more reps of the movement, rested again, and then did ten more reps of the same movement.

4. A *module* is a collection of exercises that work a specific area of the body, hence "waist module" or "hip module."

5. A *routine* is the collection of exercises that you actually perform during any given workout.

6. A *workout* is just that: a working out of the muscles with various exercises during a finite length of time (for instance, you might do a twenty-minute workout on Mondays, Wednesdays, and Fridays).

7. Put all the routines together and you have a total *program* of exercises, geared to solve your particular problems.

So, if your problem areas are the hips and the waist, you'll want to develop a *program* that utilizes the *exercises* in the hip and waist *modules*, for a collection of *routines* to be followed in a series of *workouts*, during which you will do one or more *sets* of a certain number of *reps* of a particular exercise. Got it? Read it over once more. It all makes sense, although it may seem unfamiliar to you right now. Again, don't worry about all these new words and concepts. In no time they will simply become a part of your new vocabulary.

The next step is to find out how much weight to use in each exercise. That's easy.

For each one of these basic exercises, you should use an amount of weight with which you can comfortably do the repetitions listed, that is, about 10 to 12 reps to start off with. If you have to strain and groan to do 10 reps of the squat with the bar and two 10-pound plates, then drop the weight down to 5-pound plates, or even the bar alone. It is important to do all the exercises, to get yourself a little winded, to work up a sweat, and to feel that you have really gone through a workout when you finish. You don't want to feel knocked out. You want to feel good.

There is no way on earth to tell you arbitrarily how much weight to use. You have to experiment and find that out for yourself. So, don't get upset if the first couple of workouts are spent more in finding out what you can do than in concentrating on doing the exercises.

It is very important to do the requisite number of reps. This is the only way that you can assure yourself of a good workout. So, drop the poundages to what you can work with. It's better to do ten reps with twenty pounds than to do three reps with sixty pounds. We aren't trying to train for the Olympics here, we're just trying to tone up, condition, and do some basic shaping of large areas of the body.

If the weight is too heavy to do ten reps with, then drop the weight until you have something that you *can* do ten reps with. If ten reps with a particular weight seems ridiculously easy, then increase the poundage until it's not quite so ridiculous.

Seriously, work for your best performance, but always with the number of repetitions prescribed and with good form in the exercise. As you get into the fifth week, you will begin to do two sets instead of only one. During the ninth week, you'll add weight. How much weight? Exactly the amount with which you can do the number of reps listed on the chart in the next chapter. Nothing really complicated about it.

We would have you add weight more often if this were a program designed to increase strength quickly. Instead, it's a fat-burning program, and accordingly, we have you increase sets instead of weight as the first change in the routine. Then we have you add weight when you are able to do high repetitions with two sets. The extra set helps you to add weight to the barbell while keeping up the high repetitions necessary to burn the fat. You can go as high as 6 to 8 sets on all the exercises if you need to stick with the program that long. Also, we've designed the program so that it's not too strenuous for the nonathlete. If you have experience with exercise, you'll know where you can add weight, reps, *and* sets for the maximum benefit possible.

Let's move now to the preliminary stretching and limbering exercises, so you can learn how to warm up before launching into the weight training program.

PRELIMINARY STRETCHING AND LIMBERING

Never begin a workout without warming up first. Among the best warmup exercises are the ones done at the beginning of every Karate workout. In Karate practice, a fully focused punch, strike, block, or kick can literally rip a muscle loose from its attachment when the technique is done correctly but the muscles are not warmed up. Thus, it is of extreme importance that the *Karatekas* be supple, relaxed, and warmed up before they begin a full-strength workout. The stretching exercises described below are the ones done before a Karate workout. They don't require any weights. Do them and you won't pull your muscles. For some of you, if you are just beginning, the limbering and stretching exercises themselves will be workout enough in the early days.

I • RELAX

Stand erect but relaxed, with the feet shoulder-width apart and the arms by the sides. You've done the psyching up ritual described in Chapter Three, so now relax until you feel the tension leaving you.

II • NECK

1. If your neck is stiff, practice every day with this exercise. Roll your head forward until your chin is on your chest. Then roll the head backward until you feel the crunch at the back of the neck. Do five reps.

2. Do five more reps, but this time roll the head from side to side.

3. Roll the head in a circle, first to the right for five reps, then to the left. Your neck will crunch and crackle at first, but after a couple of days it will limber up. You will also be surprised at the amount of tension you can rid yourself of with this exercise.

III • SHOULDERS

Stand erect, arms by the sides. Keep the elbows locked, and swing the arms windmill fashion in two circles that are parallel to each other. Do ten circles, slowly at first, then rapidly for the last few repetitions. Then make the same kinds of circles, but in front of the body, letting the arms cross over each other as they swing. Think of the interleaving action of an eggbeater.

IV • UPPER BACK

Stand erect, and hold the arms over the head. Hands should be clasped together, elbows locked. Starting in a posture with the arms pointing straight up, arch the back and stretch the arms toward the back as far as they will go. Repeat ten times.

V • CHEST

Stand erect, holding the arms straight in front of you, palms touching. Bring the arms back sharply, keeping them straight, until they have traveled as far to the sides as they will go. Make the motion an arc that is parallel to the floor. You will feel the chest muscles stretch. Do ten repetitions.

VI • LOWER BACK

Stand erect, then bend slowly until you are as far over as your back will let you go. Your arms should be dangling down loosely toward the floor. At the bottom of the motion, try to lean over a little farther each repetition. *Don't bounce! You don't want to pop a strain in your lower back. Do all of this slowly, with no sharp movements.* Eventually, you will be able to touch your face to your knees. Don't do this one like the traditional "touch your toes," but instead relax everything but your knees and concentrate on stretching the lower back *gently.* Do ten reps.

VII • SIDES

Stand erect and hold the hands clasped overhead. With your arms straight, bend first to one side for ten reps then to the other side. As you bend, cock your hips in the direction of the movement and you will be able to feel the stretch in the side area.

VIII • ABDOMEN

Stand erect, with the right arm extended in front of you at shoulder height, palm open and toward the floor. Swing your right leg up, trying to keep the knee locked, and kick the palm of your hand. Try not to bend the back or the knee more than necessary to complete the movement. Do ten reps with the right leg, then ten reps with the left.

IX • HIPS

Sit on the floor with your legs crossed in front of you, knees up. Put the soles of your feet together and try to push your knees down to the sides with your hands. Some of you will be able to push the knees all the way down to the floor, but most people can't. Don't feel bad if you can't go all the way. The point is to stretch the muscles and tendons, not to set a record of any kind. Do ten reps.

X • BACKS OF THE KNEES

Sit on the floor, with the legs extended out in front of you, knees and feet parallel and together. Without bending the knees, reach with both hands to the toes. If you can't make it at first, keep trying. *Again, don't bounce, but do it slowly and gently.* Do ten reps.

XI • LEGS

Here's a good one. Stand erect. Now, squat down until your bottom rests on the back of your heels. While keeping your body erect, place your left hand on the floor for balance, and extend the right leg out to the side until it is straight. Be sure that the heel of the extended leg is on the floor at the end of the movement. Raise up on the left leg, shift the weight to the right leg, and drop down on the right heel, the same way you were positioned on the left heel to begin with. Alternate for ten repetitions. Don't worry if you can't do it at first. This is a hard one. It will limber up the upper legs, the backs of the knees, and your hip and pelvic area as well.

Now that you know how to warm up, let's move to the weight training exercises themselves. You know the language now, and it's time to describe the exercises that those names belong to. Let's start at the top, with the shoulders.

SECTION ONE: SHOULDERS

A woman's shoulders are part of the total picture, but they are a special part: they accentuate what the face is saying, and they translate what's said by the mind into something that is understood by the body. They frame the body, and they provide a way in which the hair can tumble and flow down to the breasts. They do all this if they're slender, straight, accented with tiny muscle lines, and if they show a little bone. Otherwise, they just sit there, accentuating not a woman's sexiness but her dissatisfaction. Ain't nothin' uglier than old fat shoulders. Let's go to work on them.

The shoulders are made up of the deltoid muscles. There are three groups of tissue: anterior, lateral and posterior. If this sounds overly bookish, forgive us but we've got to get down to specifics.

The anterior deltoid (the one in front) gets a workout when you do any movement (such as punching) that brings the upper arm up in an arc from the sides. In most ordinary arm-swinging movements, one or all of the deltoids become active. There are some exercises, however, that isolate the deltoids for maximum shaping if you want to burn off fat and tone muscle. Here they are.

A · ANTERIOR DELTOIDS
1. FORWARD RAISES

Stand erect, with the arms hanging down, holding a barbell or dumbbells in front. Slowly raise the arms, palms facing each other, keeping the elbows locked, until the barbell or dumbbells are directly overhead. Then slowly lower the arms to the starting position. Stay very light on this one, because the deltoids are easy to injure. If you've momentarily forgotten the guidelines for estimating the amount of weight you need on each exercise, refer back to page 54 of this chapter, where a detailed explanation is given.

Forward Raises

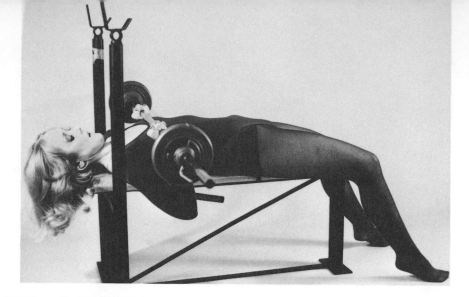

Prone Press

2. PRONE PRESS

This one is done while lying on the back. A narrow bench is necessary in order to be able to lower the barbell all the way to the chest. This exercise is sometimes called the "supine press." The movement begins with the barbell overhead on the rack. The bar should be lifted up off the rack and lowered to a position next to the chest, about four to six inches below the chin. Do not pause, but immediately extend the arms upward until the bar is in a position where it can be placed back on the supports. It is not a good idea to do this exercise without a person present to "spot" you (someone to take the weight if you are unable to extend the arms). Of all the weight training exercises, this one is one of the few that is potentially dangerous.

3. MILITARY PRESS

This exercise should begin with a barbell in position in front of and at the top of the chest, and ends with the arms extended overhead, with the bar in a position in line with the back of the head. Palms should be turned toward the front. The same exercise can be done in a seated position. This exercise shapes the upper back and the back portion of the upper arms (triceps) as well as the anterior and lateral deltoids.

Military Press

61

B • LATERAL DELTOIDS
1. LATERAL RAISES

Stand erect, arms hanging down by the sides, with a dumbbell in each hand. Slowly raise the dumbbells, keeping the elbows locked, until the arms are directly overhead. Then slowly lower the dumbbells to the starting position. CAUTION: use *light weights* in order not to pull the muscles. Also, be sure that the palms are toward the floor as you bring the dumbbells up. If you allow the hands to turn so that the palm is facing front, the anterior deltoids will come into play, thus depriving the laterals of their full workout.

Lateral Raises

Upright Rowing with Barbell

2. UPRIGHT ROWING

Stand erect, arms hanging down, holding either a barbell or two dumbbells. Slowly bring the arms up, keeping the weight(s) close to the body (*don't* swing it out, but bring it up in a straight line) until it is even with the chin. Then slowly return it to the starting position.

63

3. UPRIGHT ROWING ON A PULLEY MACHINE

Upright rowing can be duplicated on a machine especially designed for rowing motions. A pulley machine is an apparatus that consists of a handle (usually a short metal bar or a pair of handgrips) to which is attached a cable that runs through a pulley and connects to a weight at the other end. "High pulleys" are set up so you can pull the weight downward. "Low pulleys" are set up so you can pull the handle or grips straight toward you on a plane parallel to the floor. To work your deltoids, you should use the pair of handgrips instead of a bar. Most Universal Gym machines have them (a Universal Gym is an exercise machine that utilizes various kinds of pulleys and levers, all connected to a metal framework that holds weights in place). To do the exercise, grasp the handgrips with the palms out and the backs of your hands together. Hold the elbows as high as you can. Then pull the hands toward your face until they are in line with your chin. Do a few and you will feel the correct movement to work the lateral deltoids.

Upright Rowing on a Pulley Machine

65

C • POSTERIOR DELTOIDS
1. BENT BODY RAISES

Bend at the waist until your upper body is parallel to the floor. Grasp two dumbbells, remain in the bent over position and bring the dumbbells up in an arc while keeping the elbows locked. You will be able to raise your arms until they are parallel to the floor. Keep your palms toward the back. Bring the arms up in an arc that is perpendicular to the line of the bent over upper body. Don't sling or swing the weights, but do it slowly and in perfect form. Again, use a *light* weight so that you won't injure yourself. There is nothing more irritating than a shoulder injury.

If you have access to a pulley machine, you will be able to do most if not all of these shoulder exercises on it. The only thing to remember is that to exercise the muscles properly, the movements made on the pulley machine must be the same relative to the muscles themselves that are done with the free-swinging dumbbells. Remember: exercise machines are only a mechanical means of lifting weights. Their chief advantage is in their convenience. Their disadvantage is that they tend not to give strength in the joints that comes from handling free weights.

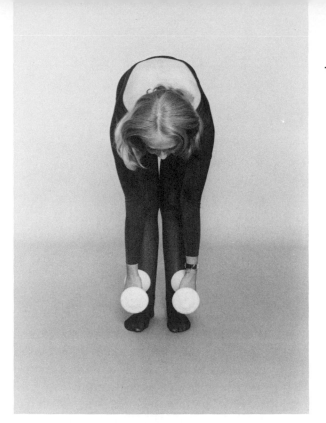

Bent Body Raises

SECTION TWO: THE BACK

A woman's back says a lot of things about her: all the things that she wants said when she wears a backless gown or a bikini. The muscles of the back form a sort of sheath over the torso, and the vitality of the body projects through the tiny ripples and lines of the back. When the movements of the shoulders are quick, the back changes like a kaleidoscope. If you've ever watched men in a room when a girl comes in wearing a backless gown, you'll know what I mean. All eyes turn if the back is as beautiful as the rest of the body.

Again, the most beautiful back is lean and active, chiseled with tiny contours and rippling like wavelets. It can be cruel (when it is turned), and it can be the invitation that all men are looking for. Given our romantic notions about the back, it seems almost a shame to talk about it in terms of muscle groups and exercises, but that's all part of the backstage preparation. It's like putting on makeup: if it's done right, it enhances without revealing the trouble you've gone to. Here are the exercises for getting your back sculptured into the shape you want.

Shoulder Shrug with Barbell

A • UPPER PORTION OF THE BACK (TRAPEZIUS)
1. SHOULDER SHRUG WITH BARBELL

Stand erect, holding a barbell in front of you, palms to the back. Slowly shrug your shoulders, and try to touch your ears with your deltoid muscles. You won't be able to, but that's the direction your shoulders should take.

2. SHOULDER SHRUG WITH DUMBBELLS

Some people get a better movement with dumbbells instead of with a barbell, since they can be held at the sides and don't pull you toward the front. Again, stand erect, this time with a dumbbell in each hand, and try to touch your ears with your shoulders.

Shoulder Shrug with Dumbbells

Rowing with Pulleys

B • MIDDLE AND LOWER PORTION OF UPPER BACK (TRAPEZIUS)

1. ROWING WITH PULLEYS

Sit on a bench facing the pulley bar. Grasp the bar with the palms facing downward. Pull the bar toward you, ending the motion with the bar at the breastbone. Use a grip that is about one shoulder width. When you do the movement, try to bunch the shoulder blades behind the back. Vary the width of the grip until you feel the best tension in the upper back.

C · THE MIDDLE BACK (LATISSIMUS DORSI)
1. ROWING WITH PULLEYS

Sit facing the pulley bar, with the bar at shoulder height or slightly above. Grasp the bar with the palms facing downward. Pull the bar to the lap. You should concentrate on working the latissimus dorsi instead of the arms. Of course, you can't rule out flexing the arm muscles completely, but with concentration you can isolate the back muscles and let them do the bulk of the work.

Rowing with Pulleys (Pull to Lap)

2. OVERHEAD PULLEY WORK

Some Universal Gym machines and almost all latissimus exercise machines provide for overhead pulley work. In this exercise, you can sit or stand with the arms raised up over the head, with the hands grasping the pulley bar. Use a wide grip and vary the grip slightly until you feel the right kind of pull in the latissimus muscles. Pull the bar downward, bringing the elbows to the sides of the body. Depending on the specific

Overhead Pulley Work (to Chest and to Neck)

portion of the lats (all the bodybuilders call the latissimus muscles "lats" for short) that you want to work, pull the bar either to the top of the chest or to the neck behind the head. Keep tension during the entire movement from overhead, down, and back up again. Keep the elbows out to the sides during the movement, and don't let them swing around to the front.

3. BENT OVER ROWING

Stand in front of a barbell, bend forward at the waist, and grasp the bar with the palms to the back. Do not straighten the body, but instead lift the bar to the abdominal area, keeping the elbows close to the sides. Another way to do this one is to straddle the bar, and then do the same movement. Be sure that you have the end of the bar up against a corner or some kind of stop so that the bar won't slide. Also, if you do it this way, you'll be grasping the bar with one hand higher than the other along the bar, since the bar will be between your legs. Either method is good. Try it both ways and choose which one suits you best. Be careful that you don't use too much weight on this one, since you will be in a bent over position with tension on the lower back as well as on the muscles of the middle back that are lifting the weight in the movement described. You may want to interleaf your fingers on the bar in a way similar to a golf club grip. It doesn't matter really, just so you do the movement correctly.

Bent Over Rowing

One-Arm Bent Over Rowing

4. ONE-ARM BENT OVER ROWING (for lower latissimus)

Bend forward at the waist, grasp a dumbbell with either hand (one at a time), and bring the elbow to the side. Try not to let the arm do all the work, but instead concentrate on letting the lower lats do the pulling. In this one, it sometimes helps to lean the unused hand against an object (such as the arm of a sofa). Stay in a bent over position throughout the exercise, bring the elbow to the side, and the dumbbell will naturally follow to a position by the side of the abdomen at the end of the movement.

D • LOWER BACK

1. STIFF-LEGGED DEAD WEIGHT LIFT

Stand erect, holding a bar in front of you, with the palms facing to the back. Slowly bend at the waist, keeping the knees stiff, until you can go no lower. Then slowly return to an erect position. This exercise is hard on the lower back, especially at first, so start off with a very light weight (maybe just the bar itself) and don't push yourself. Don't "bounce" at the bottom of the movement. Try for a stretching feeling so that you can gradually limber yourself up. When you return to the erect position, arch your back until you feel the lower back muscles flex. Hold it for a count of one, then do the whole movement again.

Stiff-Legged Dead Weight Lift

Spinal Extension

2. SPINAL EXTENSIONS

(a) Lie on the floor on your stomach. Arch your back, raising the legs and the upper body at the same time. Hold for a count of five. Work up to a count of ten or more.

(b) Get someone to hold your legs (if there is no apparatus handy) while you hang off the edge of a bench. The edge of the bench should strike you right at the pubic area. If you bruise easily, use a small flat pillow as a cushion. Let the body bend at the waist like a hinge until your face is near the floor, then slowly come back up until the body is straight. Repeat several times. Start off with the hands in front of you, and slowly work up to the point where you are able to do the movement with the hands behind the head. Eventually, you'll use a barbell plate behind your head.

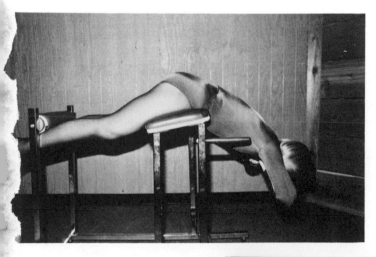

Spinal Extension on Bench

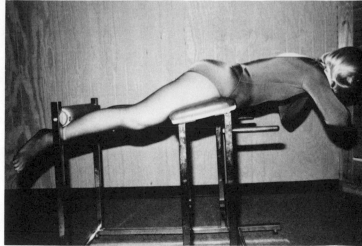

3. GOOD MORNING EXERCISE

Stand erect, with either a light bar, a barbell plate, or your hands behind the head. Lean forward until the upper body is parallel with the floor. Then return to an erect position. Use a light weight at first, so as not to injure your back. See the side lean exercises for variations on this basic back exercise.

Good Morning Exercise

SECTION THREE: THE WAIST

What's the first thing people think of when they hear "fatty"? The waist, of course, because human beings seem to store fat around the middle before it shows up anyplace else. What you don't always notice is that you are getting generally fat when the waist enlarges. That's because more of it collects around the middle than anywhere else, and it's more noticeable because there isn't much of a way that you can cover it up. A ballooning waist is a terrible thing when it gets out of control, because then it becomes a belly. Not a tummy, but a b-e-l-l-y.

People talk about their pot, their gut, their bulge, and their spare tire. Men collect fat all around their waist, ending in rolls around the sides. But for women, the real problem is usually right in front, especially since they started putting zippers on women's slacks in the front. The extra layer of cloth only serves to accentuate the problem if it has begun to develop.

Fat around the belly does something else too. It pulls your posture out of whack and causes you to droop and waddle. When that happens, it causes back trouble, pain, and generally unpleasant sensations along the spine. Furthermore, the stretch marks caused by pregnancies often are made to appear worse because of deposits of fat on the abdomen. The loose folds of stretched skin that follow pregnancy need immediate attention, and it is precisely here that some bellies get out of control and stay fat for good.

The abdomen is not all there is to the waist, however, and all your exercising should not be directed to that wad of fat on your tummy. The muscles on the sides are called the external obliques, and they collect fat like mad. Sometimes, especially when you don't go on a strict diet along with the exercises, the obliques respond quickly to work and just push the fat on further out. Women are fortunate here; for men, once that fat has collected on the obliques, it is almost impossible to get it off. Since the obliques don't get larger for women, the possibility of getting the fat off of them is enhanced. The lower back is also part of the waist, but we've already covered that area.

Now, let's get to work. First the abdominals, and then the sides. You *must* keep within the limits of your diet if you expect to lose fat around the waist. You can trim up the abs (abdominals) and obliques, but diet is really the key, diet coupled with a good fat-burning exercise routine.

A • ABDOMINALS

There is more lore about the abdominals than about any other muscle group. Some instructors advise repetitions in the hundreds; others advise the same number of reps that are used for other muscles. However, if you want to burn off fat, you should use the number of reps that will give you a burning sensation in the abdominal muscles. If that means high reps, then so be it. The abdominals adapt to workloads quickly, so you have to vary the exercises regularly. It is possible to work up to over a thousand repetitions with surprisingly little trouble if all you're doing is the regular situp.

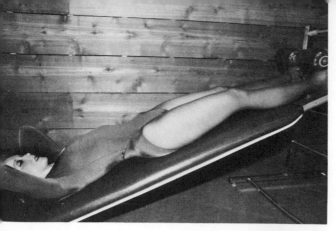

Situps (on a slant board)

1. SITUPS

Vince Gironda, the famous West Coast bodybuilding guru, maintains that situps affect the abdominals only slightly, and that the real job is done by the psoas muscles which are buried in the pelvis. He is undoubtedly right, since the purpose of the abdominals themselves is not to raise the body to a sitting position but to draw the body into a frontal arch. That is, the abdominals when flexed pull the breastbone toward the pubic bone. Situps do, however, provide overall muscle tone to the pelvic area, and thus should not be neglected. You don't need weight, but you should do situps with the knees either up toward the chest (get somebody to hold your feet or get yourself a slant board, or you can also keep your feet down by wearing iron boots), or with the knees out as if you were sitting in a lotus position. This will make the abdominals do more work, especially at the top of the movement.

2. FRONT CRUNCHES

Lie on the floor (or on a mat or a bed if you have back trouble) on your back, with your hands behind your head. Concentrate on arching the body to the front. Try to make your pubic bone touch your sternum. You won't be able to (we hope!), but that's the movement. Be sure to raise your hips slightly at the same time you raise your head and chest. Don't tense the neck, it'll just make you tired in the wrong places. Hold the contraction for a count of three. Work up to a count of ten. Try ten repetitions at first (five if you are really out of shape). Soon you will be doing sets and the fat will begin to burn off.

Front Crunches

3. LEG RAISES

(a) Hang between parallel bars (parallel bars are standard pieces of gym equipment, and consist usually of two wooden bars, mounted parallel to each other—hence the name—on stands or floor pedestals), either supporting yourself by the hands or by leaning on the elbows and forearms. Bring the legs up in front of you. Bend the knees in order to prevent back strains. Bring the legs high, but not to the point that you feel a strain in the lower back. Opinions differ among bodybuilders on leg raises. Franco Columbu, one of the top men in the world, advises quick repetitions. Others say to do it very slowly. Again, the best way is the way that allows you to feel the abs working to the maximum. Try it at various speeds, and look for the way that yields the best results.

Leg Raises (a)

Leg Raises (b)

(b) Same as above, but instead of using parallel bars use a chinning bar and hang by the hands.

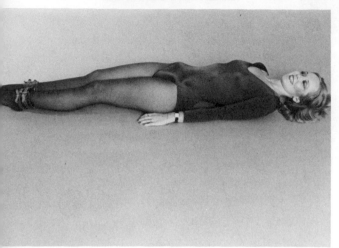

(c) Lie on the floor on your back, with the hands under the hips. Bend your knees slightly and bring the legs up to a position perpendicular to the floor, feet together.

Leg Raises (c)

(d) Same as above, but put the legs in a lotus position and combine the leg raise movement with a crunch.

Leg Raises (d)

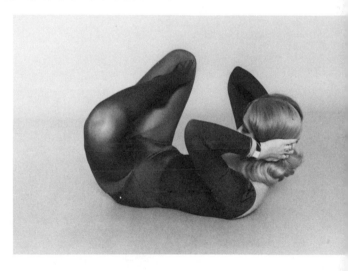

(e) When you finish the leg raises, if you really want to put the final touch on the burning, stand erect and hold on to the sides of an open doorframe for balance. Bring one leg up at a time, trying to touch your chest with your knee. You will be able to use weights on this one in a very short while. It works the area where the front of the thigh joins the abdominal area.

4. ALTERNATING LEG RAISES

(a) Use a slant board for this one. A slant board is simply a board, usually about 16 inches wide and 7 feet long, padded and covered with vinyl, which can be set up at an angle to the floor. Most slant boards have a strap or a padded bar that holds your feet in place. Lie back at about a 45-degree angle, head toward the top of the board (the high end), and bring the legs up together to the chest, bending them at the knee. Then alternate legs. This will work the area at the lower front abdominals. Be sure that the slant board is firmly placed. You can jar yourself if it slips. Don't bend the knee completely, but just enough to take the pressure off the kneecaps and the lower back.

(b) Same as above, but this time keep the knees locked straight. This will work the sides of the abdominals, for a nice hollow area between the middle of your abdomen and your sides. These exercises can be alternated with the side crunches.

Alternating Leg Raises

CAUTION: you may have a lower back problem and not even know it. If you have one, it will show up when you get on the slant board. Especially in leg raises, be careful and feel your way slowly. If it hurts your back, don't do it that way. Put heavy padding on the board, so it will give a little. Sometimes, all that's needed is a pillow (down, not foam rubber, which merely bounces you around). Also, the greater the incline of the slant board, the greater the pressure on the lower back, so take it easy at first. Certainly, you should do this one enough to get used to it before strapping ankle weights or iron boots on to augment the movement. Incidentally, the same cautionary note is suggested for doing situps on the slant board. If you have a back problem, you can aggravate it by putting so much pressure on the lower back. At the first hint of sensations other than normal muscle burning, you should slack off and put some padding under you.

B • THE SIDES (EXTERNAL OBLIQUES)
1. SIDE LEANS

This is a controversial one. If you use weight at all, use a light load. Better to put the hands behind the head and move from an erect position to the one side and then to the other, keeping the eyes to the front and the back on a vertical plane. If you have developed fat in the area directly above the hip-bones, then vary the exercise and make the movement slightly to the front instead of directly to the sides. Two sets of fifteen reps on this one and you will be able to feel a pump without any weight at all. You will be sore the following day. You'll be able to tell which area you're working out by the area that is sore. Vary the direction of the lean until you are sore in the place that you want to reduce. After the third workout, you won't be sore anymore, so enjoy the soreness while it lasts as a diagnostic tool. It's all a matter of attitude. A lot of people when they get sore think that the world has played a dirty trick on them. Think about it in a new way. Nature has provided you with an indicator that tells you where you've worked out the muscles. Relish the soreness. It's yours. It tells you where things are going right. It is you telling you what is going on.

94

Side Crunches

2. SIDE CRUNCHES

You can burn fat off the area to the sides of the abdominals by doing the crunches not directly to the front but slightly to the side. In doing this variation, try to make the lower ribs touch the junction of the leg and hip. Again, you won't succeed, but that is the movement you are after.

3. SEATED TWISTS

Sit on a bench or cross-legged on the floor, with an empty bar (or a broomstick) across your shoulders behind the neck. Stretch the arms out and grasp the bar with the hands as far toward the tips of the bar as you can reach. Relax the arms, and adjust their position so that they are not cramped or uncomfortable. Twist first to one side and then to the next. Don't try to keep count, but instead either watch a clock or use a timer (the inexpensive timers sold at photography supply shops are ideal, about five dollars), and twist for five minutes. Work up to fifteen or twenty minutes. Turn on the television, radio, or hi-fi for this one so you won't get so bored.

4. SEATED TWISTS LEANING FORWARD

A variation of the above is to lean forward about 30 degrees while you twist. You will find that you will be able to twist faster this way, and it will work out the sides of the lower back as well as the intercostals under the pectorals and arms. The purpose of twists is not to build strength but to flex the tissue around the waist, thus helping to grind the fat away and tone up the muscles. Don't expect quick results. The trick here is the cumulative effect of the exercise.

SECTION FOUR: THE HIPS

Back during World War II, Betty Grable posed for a pinup photo that was to become one of the most famous pictures of the era. You remember it: she stood with the back to the cameraman, peeking over her right shoulder. Her legs are together, and she is wearing a one-piece bathing suit. Stretch your memory a bit and try to remember what she looked like. She had no shape, really. Her legs were devoid of contour, and her hips (her fanny, actually) formed a sort of a marshmallow shape that was held together by her bathing suit. All due respects to Ms. Grable, and cheers for lifting the morale of servicemen everywhere, but today we know better. We've seen fannies in everything from Vogue to Penthouse, and we've become all too aware of the presence of unsightly fat gathered together by a corset or a tight bathing suit. There are fannies and there are fannies. The kind you want is tight and foxy, with no droop. It is squared off at the top by the pelvic bones, and there is little or no horizontal crease along the bottom. There should be a hollow at the sides, to show off your long, lean legs.

Do some research the next time you're sitting on a park bench or at a sidewalk cafe. What do the other girls look like? Watch the ones in slacks. There is a certain look that women have when they don't droop. Their legs look a foot longer, for one thing. Think about it. When your bottom sags, it can sag as much as six inches. No kidding. Let's say that you are average height, say five feet six inches. Your legs are not particularly long. If your bottom sags, you've automatically lost four to six inches of leg length. Also, the effect of a sagging bottom is to emphasize the lower part of the fanny instead of the fanny itself. You can look six inches shorter if you sag. You can look six inches taller if you don't. You aren't really shorter or taller, but the length of the legs can be visual as well as actual. Don't let the fanny sag and you will look taller. It really works.

With a small, tight fanny also comes a sleek look in slacks. You can see space between your legs at the highest point. If you trim your hips on top, and do away with the droop on the bottom, you will look lean, quick, narrow, and young. Think of the hips not merely as your fanny. Think about the top, the sides, and the bottom. There should be hollows on the sides, and there should be no "riding pants" effect at the bottom sides to spoil the line of a lean leg. You should be able to wear slacks that are tight from proper tailoring instead of from barely being able to stretch over the fat. The bones should show and the muscles should define the shape of the entire area. You shouldn't have to rely on the miracles of bias-cut stretchy girdles, but instead on the miracle of good health and shapely muscle. What you want to do is make sure that the total area is in shape. Think small. Think narrow. Think of the shanks of young mares, or of deer in the forest.

While you're thinking about it, here are the exercises that will give you what you want.

BODYSCULPTURE

A • HIGH HIPS
1. LEG SWINGS

This movement should be performed with the toe pointed. Swing the right leg, toe pointed, as high in front and behind as you can, tracing a straight line with the leg and foot. You will probably start with no weight at all and add an ankle weight later. Repeat with the left leg. This one loosens up the hip joints, and makes you supple and agile.

Leg Swings

Reclining Hip Rolls

2. RECLINING HIP ROLLS

When you finish the seated twists, lie on your back on the floor, pull your knees up above you, grasping the lower legs with the hands (put the lower legs in a loose lotus position), and roll the hips from one side to the other while keeping the upper body flat on the floor. In other words, keep the upper body immobile, while you twist at the waist, thus rolling the hips back and forth. This exercise will massage the back and tops of the hips and sides, as well as strengthen the external obliques. If you arch your body forward, you can combine this exercise with abdominal crunches while massaging the lower back. Start with five minutes and work up to fifteen.

3. LATERAL LEG RAISES

Stand erect, holding on to a doorframe or a high bench. Raise the leg in an arc to the side, keeping the knee locked. The leg should go as high as your hip joint will allow it to go. Be sure that the arc is directly to the side.

Lateral Leg Raises (Standing)

Lateral Leg Raises (Lying on Side)

A variation would be to lie on the side, raising the leg in an arc. This one will exercise the area to the sides that makes the nice hollow we talked about earlier.

Posterior Leg Raises

4. POSTERIOR LEG RAISES

Stand erect, same as in the lateral leg raises. Raise the leg to the back in an arc, keeping the knee locked. This exercise works the area where the leg joins the back of the hip.

NOTE: in both of these exercises, you will be able to use ankle weights or iron shoes after a few weeks.

5. X-RATED HIP EXERCISE

Why "X-rated"? Okay: lie on your back, with your knees bent slightly outward, feet flat on the floor as close to the buttocks as you can comfortably get them. Keep your shoulders on the floor, arch the back, and push your pelvis toward the ceiling. At the top of the movement, hold for a count of one while clinching the buttocks. This will work the area in the back of the hips at the junction of the legs and the hips. It gets at the droop. You can vary the area of the hips being worked out by varying the position of the feet. Try it with feet together for a few reps, then try it with the feet wide apart. You will be able to feel the difference.

X-Rated Hip Exercise

B · MIDDLE HIPS
1. LATERAL LEG RAISES (see page 102).
2. RECLINING HIP ROLLS (see page 101).
3. LUNGES

Stand erect, step forward a giant step with either foot, dropping into a position such that the stepping leg is bent at the knee, thigh parallel to the floor, while the stationary leg is straight and stretched out to the back. This exercise performs a number of functions. It stretches the muscles in the hips and the legs, it strengthens the top and outer portion of the front thigh, and it makes the ankles more flexible. Some weightlifters use heavy weights in this one, because it is a training exercise for the "split style" legwork in the Olympic lifts.

Lunges

C • LOWER HIPS
1. LUNGES (see preceding page)
2. BACK LEG EXTENSION

Kneel on the floor, with the arms extended and the hands on the floor slightly more than shoulder width apart, supporting your upper body. Your knees will be bent at a 90-degree angle, and your body should be parallel to the floor. Bring the right knee forward and try to touch your chest with it (bend the knee to keep from scraping the floor with the top of your foot), then extend the leg backward until it is completely straight in line with the body and parallel to the floor. Do several repetitions, then change to the left leg. This exercise works the area where the leg joins the pelvis both in the front and in the back.

Back Leg Extension

Excess Baggage Roll

3. EXCESS BAGGAGE ROLL

Another kind of hip roll helps to massage the fat off the lower hips. Sit cross-legged on the floor and roll from side to side. This will help to break down the "excess baggage" that you have collected at the junction of the hips and the back of the thighs. Try fifteen minutes of this one. It helps to do this one in conjunction with leg curls, which are described on pages 131–32.

D • TOTAL HIPS: KNEE POSITIONS FOR THE SQUAT

The squat works the entire hip area and you should vary the direction of the knees in order to get the full benefit of the exercise. By keeping the knees and feet together, the area along the bottom of the buttocks is brought into play. By pointing the knees outward and keeping the feet wide apart, the area at the side of the hips is worked. Try sets with both and you will feel the area being worked. Try to work the area under which you have the greatest layer of fat, thus striving for symmetry. Now that we have the knee positions for the squat described, let's go on to a description of the squat (or "kneebend" as it is sometimes called).

1. HALF SQUATS

In this variation of the squat, hold a barbell across the shoulders and drop down until the upper legs are parallel to the floor. Don't use too heavy a weight until you know your limitations, or you might drop past the point of no return and wind up sprawled on the floor with a weight around your neck that you can't get off. Ralph did just that about three years ago, and wound up with an injured knee and a cracked rib (he was using 300 pounds).

Half Squats

2. FULL SQUATS

These can be done either flatfooted or on the toes. If you do them flatfooted, simply drop all the way down (gently) until your buttocks are touching the heels. If you do them the other way, place a book or a block of wood (preferably wood, since the bindings break on books) under the heels, then drop to the backs of the heels the same way as in the flatfooted squat. Either way you do it, keep the back straight (don't lean forward more than you have to in order to keep your balance), and keep your head up, looking straight ahead. Don't allow your shoulders to drop or your head to bow down. It's best to use a rack from which the bar may be taken, especially if you are using heavy weights. If you are using light weights (which you should at first), you will have no trouble lifting the bar from the floor to the back of the neck. When you lift it, be sure to start from a position in which the knees are bent and the upper body is parallel to the floor. Then, as you raise up, straighten the legs and pull the weight up at the same time. If you coordinate your movements correctly, you will end up with the bar in front of you, resting at the top of your chest. Then "bounce" it over your head until it rests on the shoulders. With a little practice, you will be able to do the entire movement in one sweep.

Full Squats

SECTION FIVE: THE THORACIC AREA

Although some people think of Tarzan or King Kong when they hear the words "chest exercises," let's use it for shorthand so we won't have to say "thoracic area" every time we describe an exercise for the upper frontal portion of the torso. The thoracic area for women is the area of the breasts, and that's what's important about the area, both for the women who have and the men who look.

The ideal breast is soft but firm. It doesn't sag, and it doesn't flop. It's not uncomfortable when you run, and it is not so big and puffy that you have to harness yourself up to keep it from touching your belly. That's the ideal breast according to current fashion. Twenty years ago, we all wanted breasts to be bigger than any sane person would think possible. Even *Playboy* has gotten away from this notion, although Little Annie Fanny still looks like somebody has been after her with an air hose.

When women think about pectoral exercises, they are usually thinking about making their breasts either jut further out (with the development of larger pectorals) or firming their breasts up by getting rid of the extra fat that causes them to droop. Let's talk for a few minutes about both of these ideas, and see what truth there is to either of them.

In the first place, since you as a woman will not be able to build huge pectoral muscles, you may as well forget about

building up an internal breast augmentation by muscle mass. You can't develop internal falsies. But you can tone up the pectoral muscles to the point that the breasts become much firmer than they probably are now. How does this work? Simple. By doing pectoral exercises, you can awaken the muscles, trim off the fat around the breasts, and define more sharply what you already have.

Firmness is the thing to strive for, not size. You can indeed firm up the breasts with exercise. You might even push them out a little bit, especially if you are totally undeveloped in the thoracic area. If your breasts are naturally small, you can accentuate them by cleaning up the fatty tissue around them. If your breasts are naturally large, you can reduce the fatty content by dieting and exercise, thus producing a firm, shapely breast instead of a puffy, oversized one. If your breasts tend to droop, you can arrest the droop and stop it from going any further by toning up the muscles to which the breasts are attached. Any way you look at it, pectoral exercises will improve the appearance of your breasts, and enable you to wear all of those skimpy outfits that you've been wanting to wear all this time.

Now that we have defined our goals (if not named the area), let's be a bit more precise and identify the specific areas of the thorax. And let's go ahead and use the word "chest" as we outline exercises for these muscles, and see how they work for maximum progress.

BODYSCULPTURE

A • UPPER PECTORALS
1. INCLINE PRESS
This exercise is done the same as the prone press but with an incline bench so that it will work the upper pectorals. See the description of the prone press in Section One, A2 (page 60). The incline press can be done with either a barbell or dumbbells.

B • CENTRAL AND MIDDLE PECTORALS
1. PRONE PRESS
See Section One, A2 (page 60). To concentrate on the pectorals, use a wide grip on the bar and a weight that you can lift for 12 to 15 reps. You can use a barbell or a pair of dumbbells.

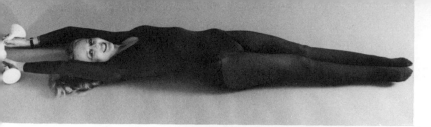

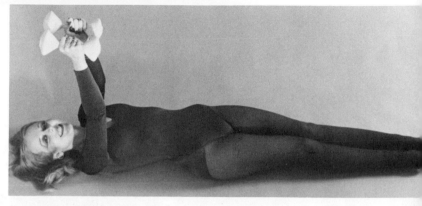

2. STRAIGHT ARM PULLOVERS

Lie on the back, with a (very) light weight held overhead at arm's length. A barbell plate will do, as long as it's light (5 pounds at first, or less). Keep the arms straight, and bring them down in an arc until they are parallel to the floor and are extended to a position that would be over the head if you were standing erect. Inhale deeply as you bring the arms down. When in the downmost position, stretch the chest by arching the back slightly. Then bring the arms up, still keeping the elbows locked, and exhale on the way up. Inhale as you let the arms down again, expanding the chest as far as it will go. This exercise will build up the lower pectorals and will also (and primarily) expand the rib cage. It will also help you get rid of the "office desk slump" that hides your breasts between sagging shoulders. Get an extra stretch by lying on a bed with the shoulders at the edge, so you can bring the extended arms even lower at the end of the downward movement.

3. BENT ARM PULLOVERS

Same as number (2) above, but this time bend the arms at the elbows. Now it becomes a latissimus as well as a pectoral exercise. Be careful that you don't hit yourself on the top of the head. In the downmost position, the upper arms should be roughly parallel to the floor, and the forearms should be perpendicular to the floor. Inhale and exhale during the movements as described above.

4. FLYES (short for "flying exercise")

Lie on your back. Hold two light dumbbells directly over the chest, arms extended straight, palms facing each other. Keep the arms straight, and let them down to either side until they are parallel to the floor. Then bring them to the upright position again. This will trim the portion of the pectorals that makes a vertical line down the center of the chest. The effect for women will be a fine sculpturing of the center of the thorax between the breasts. You can vary the exercise by using an incline bench (a prone press bench that hinges up so that you can lie on it with your body bent upward at the hips

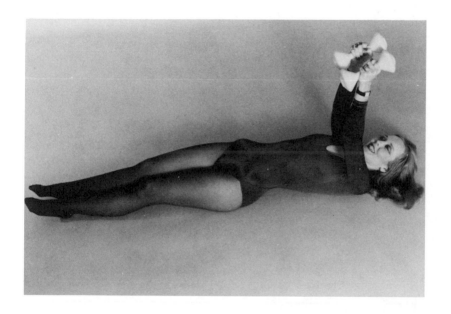

and waist) or a decline bench (the same thing, but made so that you can lie with the head lower than the feet). The incline bench flyes will work the upper pectorals, while the decline bench will work the lower area of the thorax. Further, you can do the flyes either with straight arms or with bent arms. You will be able to handle more weight with bent arms; you will find a light weight more than enough if you keep the arms straight. One note of caution: when doing straight-arm flyes, you will lock the elbows. If you have any old tennis injuries, you may feel a twinge. Keep with a light weight and you shouldn't have any problems.

C • LOWER PECTORALS
1. STRAIGHT ARM PULLOVERS (see page 115)
2. BENT ARM PULLOVERS (see page 115)
3. DECLINE PRESS

Not a popular one, but a variation on the theme, this time for the lower pecs. If it is an uplift that you need the most, try this one. Lie on a decline bench or backwards on an incline bench (see photo) so that your head is down instead of up. Use a barbell or dumbbells. Do exactly the same movement for the decline press that you would do for the prone press or incline press: push the weight straight up in a line perpendicular to the floor. Because of the angle of the body to the movement of the exercise, you will work a different area of the pectorals: the lower edge.

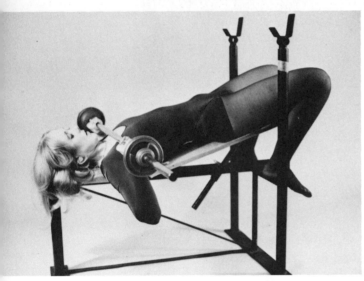

Decline Press

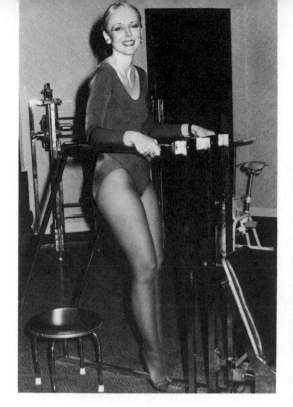

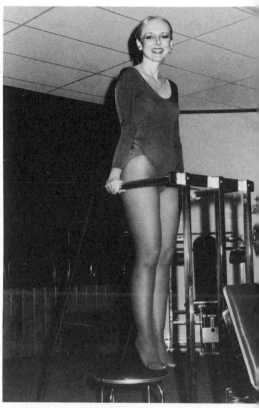

Parallel Bar Dip

4. PARALLEL BAR DIPS

This exercise can be done either on a parallel bar setup or, if none is available, on the arms of a sturdy chair. If you do them on the arms of a chair, let the legs go to the front, resting the heels on another chair. Be careful if you use chairs. Don't put them on a slick surface, or they'll slide. Start off with the arms straight, hands gripping the parallel bar or the arms of the chair. If you use a parallel bar, you can let your legs hang down between the bars. Slowly bend the arms at the elbow and lower yourself down until you can't go any farther. Then slowly raise yourself back up again. This is a toughie, and you had probably better begin by helping with the legs a little bit. To do this, put a footstool between the bars or do it on a chair so that your legs are resting in front of you on another chair, thus subtracting part of their weight from the load on your arms. This one will work the lower pectorals (the underside of the breast), and it is also a good arms exercise for the triceps (the back of the upper arms).

SECTION SIX: THE ARMS

Not many people think about arms when they talk about feminine beauty. Arms sort of get taken for granted, especially since for a long time it hasn't been necessary for women to think of themselves as potentially strong. There is a lot of mythology about women's arms, as there is about so many portions of the female anatomy. Years ago, pregnant women were told not to reach upward to hang out clothes, for fear of causing the umbilical cord to become tangled around the neck of the fetus. Women have been described as "poor weak creatures who give you all they got" (*Zorba the Greek*). This usually means that a man can grab a woman's wrists and hold her down (or up, depending on your perspective). The first line of feminine weakness is usually the arms: it's what they grab you by to keep you from clawing at them.

Your arms don't have to be weak. That doesn't mean that they have to be huge to be strong, either. You just have to exercise them, and stop believing that you have to be weak because you are a woman.

There's more to it than that, of course, because we don't think of brawn when we think of a woman's arms. A woman's strength is often in her subtlety, and when a beautiful arm is properly used, it carries more power than all the weightlifters in the world. Ask any man, regardless of the strength of his biceps, who has just been gently but definitely pushed away. There's more force in that simple movement than in all the iron pushing at the Olympics.

Let's talk about the bad side for a few minutes. Nobody wants a pair of flabby arms. Nobody wants to look as if they've run up a sail every time they raise their arms. It has nothing to do with men. It has to do with self-esteem. It has to do with what *you* want to look like. And you don't want shapeless, flabby, puffy, weak arms. They don't look good, and they can ruin the effect that you are trying to achieve. What you want is a pair of arms that are symmetrically formed, and help you to show off a lean, quick, beautiful figure. Here are the exercises to help you get what you want.

A • UPPER ARMS

The upper arm is divided into two muscle groups, the triceps and the biceps. The function of the biceps is to pull the hand toward the body. Most biceps exercises are called "curls." The function of the triceps is to push the hand away from the body. Most triceps exercises are called "presses" or "extensions." All of these exercises will shape and strengthen the arms.

1. THE CURL

Curls can be done in a variety of ways. You can use dumbbells, a barbell, or an exercise machine.

(a) STANDING CURL (sometimes called "military" curl)

Stand erect; hold a barbell or two dumbbells in front of you, resting against the front of your thighs. Keep the elbows against the sides, and raise the weight in an arc until the bar stops against the upper chest. Keep yourself from cheating by propping the elbows against the sides of the abdomen. The exercise should be done with a smooth motion, returning the bar to the thighs at the same rate of speed at which it was brought to the chest. The palms should be facing upwards.

Standing Curl

Scott Bench Curl

(b) SCOTT BENCH CURL

This curl is also known as the "Preacher Stand" Curl, and was named after Mr. Olympia, Larry Scott, one of the greatest bodybuilders of all time. It consists of a slanted square board on which you place the elbows, and which keeps you from cheating on the motion of the curl. In this exercise, the elbows are propped against the bench, and the weights are brought in an arc to a position in front of the shoulders, palms up, then returned to the straight arm position. You should place your elbows high on the bench. You may want to use extra padding under the elbows.

(c) PULLEY CURLS

These are also effective. In these exercises, the pulley bar replaces the barbell or dumbbell, and is pulled toward the body. If you want to develop the lats (latissimus muscles) at the same time that you are working the biceps, bring the bar to a position near your lap. If you want to develop the upper back at the same time that you are working the biceps, pull the bar toward the middle of your chest. Palms should be turned up if you are going to work the biceps, down if you want to work the inner portion and the sides of the biceps. You can work the inner or outer head of the biceps by using a wide or a narrow grip on the barbell.

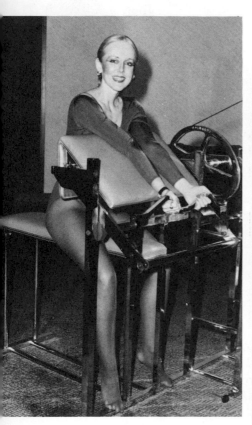

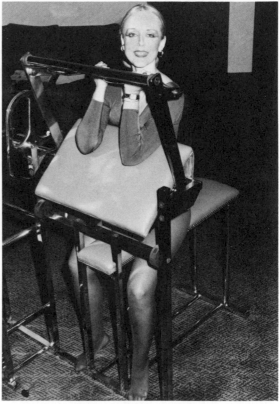

Pulley Curls

French Curl

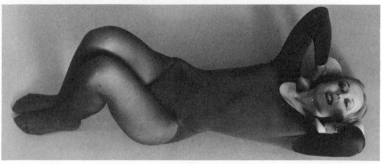

2. THE PRESS
(a) MILITARY PRESS   See Section One, A3 (page 61).
(b) BEHIND THE NECK PRESS

The behind the neck press is similar to the military press, except that the movement begins with the bar behind the head, resting on the trapezius muscles and the shoulders. This exercise allows you to concentrate on the shoulders while working the triceps.

(c) PRONE PRESS   See Section one, A2 (page 60).

3. FRENCH CURL

Where did the name come from? Probably some Frenchman invented the exercise. Lie on your back on the prone press bench (or on the floor), hold the weights straight up as if you were going to do a prone press. Instead of bringing the weights down to your chest, bring them in an arc down to a position at the top of the head. Do this movement without changing the position of the elbows. Obviously, this exercise utilizes light weight, else you might accidentally bop yourself on the top of your head! Also, some people find that French curls hurt their elbows, so take it easy at first. Be sure to do the movement with strict form, else the value of the exercise will be lost. This one is a real toner and definer, and will lean out the back of your arms like no other exercise.

B · FOREARMS

It's rare that forearms are a problem for women, but if you have fatty folds or want to strengthen your forearms, try any movement that involves holding a weight in your hands while rotating them at the wrists. One of the best exercises is the "wrist roll," in which you sit down on a bench, grasp a dumbbell bar with both hands, and bend the wrists up and down. You'll feel the tightening in the forearms very quickly. Another method is to drill a hole in a two-inch-diameter short rod, run a rope through the hole, and attach a barbell plate to the other end of the rope. Knot the end at the rod so it won't pull through. Then roll the rod so that the rope winds up around the rod. When it is fully wound, unwind it. You'll be surprised at how quickly the forearms get tired. A third method involves any squeezing movement of the hands. Twist a towel until it won't twist any further, or squeeze a rubber ball in the palm of the hands. All of these movements work the forearms, and all of them will tell you immediately how out of shape your forearms are. The forearms will give you a burning sensation, just like the calves do when you really work them out.

SECTION SEVEN: THE LEGS

Everybody looks at legs. Men, for obvious reasons. Women look at women's legs to compare, to check out the competition, to see how new boots and new hose look, to see how new outfits complement the natural beauty of all those lean, leggy girls. We've always been fascinated by legs. Beginning (in the U.S.) about 1963, fashion went leggy, and you were nothing unless you had the kind of legs ordinarily associated with adolescent girls. Twiggy brought with her a new ideal leg: skinny, shapeless, and long. Boot manufacturers designed footwear that could not be worn by anyone with a well-developed leg. Women tried to get rid of their leg muscles. Girls in North Dakota discovered to their dismay that by leaving exposed flesh between their boot tops and their miniskirts, they developed fatty tissue around their knees from the subzero cold. Legs were sleek, silvery, webbed, figured, and came in all colors of sheer.

But it was next to impossible for women to get the New Legs unless they were born with them. Women's magazines ran hundreds of articles on reducing the legs. Most of the exercises were worthless unless you were naturally thin and had simply allowed yourself to get a trifle out of shape. People worried about doing heavy exercises for fear of producing a heavy, muscular leg. Muscles were out. Size was out. Shape was out. An awful lot of women wore miniskirts who shouldn't have.

There would never have been such a successful campaign to show off legs if they weren't interesting to look at to begin with. There is nothing more appealing, more breathtaking, more fascinating, more inspiring, than beautiful legs. A long, lean, well-contoured thigh, a trim knee, a gently swelling calf, a narrow ankle: they are all a joy to behold.

Your legs are shaped by three things: bone structure, muscle tissue, and fatty tissue. Unless you have some sort of genuine medical abnormality, your legs have all the requisite muscles, in all the right places. A shapely leg is one that is defined by the muscles that make it up. If the shape of your leg is defined by fat, then the natural contour will be lost. All women have a layer of adipose tissue over their muscles. That's part of being a woman. That's why women have curves. You can't get rid of all the fat on your legs, and you don't really want to. What you want to do is tone up the muscles of the leg, get rid of extra fatty deposits on the calf and around the knee, and rout out that layer that collects on the outside of the thighs below the hips. If you do a good job of exercising the leg muscles, the unsightly hollow bow that even the trim models have between their thighs will round out with shapely muscle.

You should have a lean thigh, with a well-defined contour on the front inside area, defined by the muscle that ends at the top of the knee. On the outside of the thigh, especially at the point where the leg joins the hip, women tend to collect lumps of cellulite. This should be slimmed to the point that there is only the suggestion of a break in the line when you are standing with your feet together. If you stand with the feet and the knees together, there should be no space between the thighs; however, the thighs should touch only lightly in this area. Any more will be a bulge.

The knees should be trim, with no layer of fat sagging on the inside. Further, there should be no sagging fat behind the knees to detract from the natural contour of the back of the leg. There should be a gentle swell of calf, narrowing down to a slender ankle that shows some bone. If it is all put together the right way, you should be able to trace a line from the waist to the knee, then to the ankle. You should be able to trace another line from the front and side of the pelvis down to the knee, a curve around the knee, then another graceful line swelling then narrowing to the ankle. When you look at the leg from the side, there should be no overhang from the knee-cap. Also, the back of the thigh should swoop up into the fanny, not be cut off by a horizontal overhang.

That's the perfect leg. Not only from our point of view, but from the perspective of the best contemporary photographers of high-fashion models. We can't delude ourselves about the beauty of a leg that is shaped like a pole. We've become too sophisticated about our bodies for that. The best models have beautiful legs, and they don't have to be wearing knee-length boots to get by.

Now, let's go over the exercises for the legs. Try to think of your legs as bigger versions of your arms. For legs, you do leg presses, leg curls, and calf raises. The presses are analogous to those done with the arms: in them, you extend the legs until they are straight. In the curls, you bring the straightened leg up until it is fully bent at the knee. The calf raises are similar to a variety of wrist curls that are done to strengthen the forearms. Of course, there are many variations of these basic movements, each designed to rout out fat and/or build up muscle tissue in specific places.

A • UPPER LEGS
1. LEG EXTENSIONS

Sit on a bench, with the knees bent and the lower legs dangling perpendicular to the floor. The edge of the bench should be under the knees. You might want to put a thin cushion under the legs at the edge if the bench has no padding. Raise the lower legs until the knees are locked and the legs are parallel to the floor. This exercise works the muscles directly above the knee on the inside of the leg. You can use iron shoes, ankle weights, or a leg extension machine for this one.

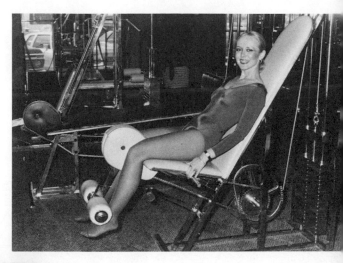

Leg Extensions

129

2. LEG PRESSES (to be done on a leg press machine)

Sit in the chair and push the weight up with the feet until the legs are straight. Don't lock the knees, else you might injure them. Use a machine for this one. *Don't* try to balance a barbell on the bottoms of your feet. This one works the muscles in the middle and to the outside of the thigh.

Leg Presses

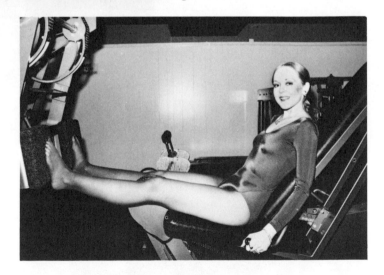

3. SQUATS OR KNEEBENDS
(a) HALF SQUATS   See Section Four, D1 (page 109).
(b) FULL SQUATS   See Section Four, D2 (page 110).

4. LEG CURLS
(a) LEG CURLS ON A MACHINE

Lie on the stomach, hook the feet under the padded bar, and bring the legs from a straight position to a fully bent position so that the feet are over your buttocks. This exercise works the muscles on the back of the thighs, and also helps burn off the fat at the junction of the thighs and the lower hips.

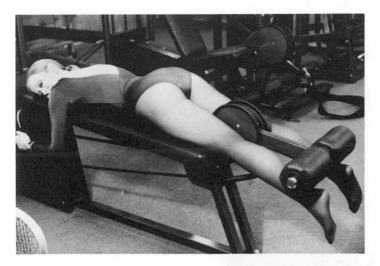

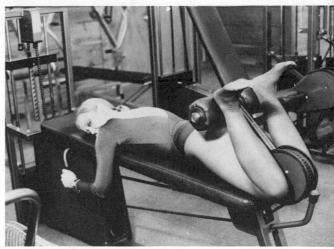

Leg Curls on a Machine

(b) LEG CURLS WITHOUT A MACHINE

If you don't have access to a leg curl machine, then get a pair of iron boots, fasten them to your feet, and stand in a doorway with the front of the leg against the doorframe. Alternately lift the feet from the floor to as high a point as they will go. Try to touch the back of the thigh with your heel. Do several reps with one leg, then several with the other. Don't lift both feet at the same time, unless you have an unnaturally strong grip on the doorframe!

(c) LEG CURLS WITH A LITTLE HELP FROM YOUR FRIENDS

Get someone to hold your feet behind the heels and apply resistance as you lie on your stomach. Try to lift your feet up in the same motion that you would use if you were using the leg curl machine. Regardless of the way that you perform the exercise, you won't need much weight. You will be surprised at how little resistance is needed to give the backs of your legs all the workout they need.

B • LOWER LEGS

1. CALF RAISES

There are many ways to perform calf raises. Some machines are designed so that you rise on your toes pushing upward against a padded weight holder that rests on the tops of your legs or knees. Other machines require that you dip under padded braces that fit on top of your shoulders. Still another type of machine uses a strap that circles the pelvis at the waist and which is attached to a chain that is attached to a clasp that is hooked to a weighted cable. A great deal of complication just to get the calves working! You can also hold a barbell on your shoulders and rise on your toes while balancing the barbell. Another variation is to lean over a chair or bench, let someone sit on your back, and rise on your toes against the weight of the person sitting on your hips. This is called the "donkey raise," because the helper is astride your back as if he or she were riding a donkey.

Calf Raises

Whatever method you use, there are three basic ways to hold the feet: toes pointed outward, toes pointed inward or feet parallel. Each position works a slightly different portion of the calf. For maximum results, do all three.

133

2. ANKLE ROTATIONS

This exercise massages and tones the tissue around the ankles. Lie first on your stomach, then (for the next set) on the back, and rotate your feet. You should wear either iron boots or some strap-on ankle weights for this one.

Ankle Rotations

Calf Flexes

3. CALF FLEXES

After you finish the rise on toes exercises, take a few minutes to shift the weight while standing from one foot to the other, each time pointing the foot and cramping the calf muscle when you do. This will burn the fat off, and make the rise on toes exercises more effective. Do about twenty reps with each leg.

That's the description of the exercises. Now that you know how to do them, you can combine them in the modules that are described in the next chapter. If you've read the exercises carefully, you will have no trouble working out in any of the modules. Look at the illustrations for the exercises, and try to visualize the proper way to do them. In many cases, your body will tell you when you are doing things right.

CHAPTER 5

The Exercise Program: How to Develop Your Own Program Uniquely Tailored to Your Needs

What's coming now is in some ways the simplest part of the book. We've compiled all the exercises, and we've got our heads and our bodies ready for the task of Bodysculpture that lies before us. What's left to do is to decide on a regular exercise program and what goes into it.

There are over sixty exercises in the total list in Chapter Four. You're probably wondering, "Do I have to do them all?"

The answer is *no*. Our reason for listing so many exercises and putting them together in this way is that it allows you to find the specific exercises among all those listed that are most applicable to your specific problem areas. You can look over your body, identify the areas in which you have problems, then search through the list of exercises and see easily which one works those areas. The list covers every body area. Wherever you have a problem, we've got an exercise for it.

If you think about it, all of this makes perfect sense, and it's the key to the whole Bodysculpture idea. You don't need someone standing over you all the time telling you which exercise to do for what. All you need is a list of exercises, descriptions of how to do them, and an objective look at your particular set of problems. That's what the figure analysts at the health spas do anyway, and there is no reason for you to have to pay the middleman his high fee. If you can see the problem and if you can locate the exercises that are relevant to that problem, then you are already more than halfway to solving it. If you have an easy way to find the solutions, an automatic way to locate your relevant exercises, then you don't have to depend on anybody else, and that's the way that real independence is enjoyed.

So let's begin. Your first step is to get a good tape measure and a mirror, preferably a full-length one. Take a good hard look at yourself. Then measure with your tape the following areas: bust, midriff, waist, hips, thighs, knees, calves, ankles, wrists, upper arms. Get a small notebook and record each measurement you've taken. Don't squeeze the tape measure to make the measurement smaller. Just lay it snugly along the skin and record what you find.

How do you know when a measurement is too large? The old rule that hips and bust should be approximately the same is a rough and ready guide. The waist should be at least ten inches smaller, and the thighs five to six inches smaller than your waist. Calves should be six to seven inches smaller than the thighs, and the ankles should be from four to five inches smaller than the calf. Where do these figures come from? From almost every magazine you can find that has an article on symmetry. The proportions are purely arbitrary, and you shouldn't go off the wall if you don't tally up to the norm. On the other hand, if your measurements are grossly out of whack with these norms, then you've probably discovered a problem area.

The purpose of the taping is twofold: it'll give you a baseline for improvements and it will also help you to be honest in your appraisal of your problems. Now look in the mirror. Check yourself out from all angles. Is there dimpled fat on the back of the buttocks or thighs? Does your tummy bulge when you stand at ease? Is there a spare tire at your midriff? A

1 S&L 10 REPS 1 SET	**2** S&L 12 REPS 1 SET	**3** S&L 15 REPS 1 SET	**4** OFF	**5** GC 10 REPS 1 SET	**6** OFF	**7** GC 10 REPS 1 SET
8 OFF	**9** GC 12 REPS 1 SET	**10** OFF	**11** GC 12 REPS 1 SET	**12** OFF	**13** GC 14 REPS 1 SET	**14** OFF
15 GC 14 REPS 1 SET	**16** OFF	**17** GC 16 REPS 1 SET	**18** OFF	**19** GC 16 REPS 1 SET	**20** OFF	**21** GC 18 REPS 1 SET
22 OFF	**23** GC 20 REPS 1 SET	**24** OFF	**25** GC 12 REPS 2 SETS	**26** OFF	**27** GC 12 REPS 2 SETS	**28** OFF
29 W&H 10/20 REPS 2 SETS	**30** OFF	**31** GC 14 REPS 2 SETS	**32** OFF	**33** W&H 10/20 REPS 2 SETS	**34** OFF	**35** GC 14 REPS 2 SETS
36 OFF	**37** W&H 12/22 REPS 2 SETS	**38** OFF	**39** GC 16 REPS 2 SETS	**40** OFF	**41** W&H 12/22 REPS 2 SETS	**42** OFF
43 GC 16 REPS 2 SETS	**44** OFF	**45** W&H 14/24 REPS 2 SETS	**46** OFF	**47** GC 18 REPS 2 SETS	**48** OFF	**49** W&H 14/24 REPS 2 SETS
50 OFF	**51** GC 18 REPS 2 SETS	**52** OFF	**53** W&H 16/26 REPS 2 SETS	**54** OFF	**55** GC 20 REPS 2 SETS	**56** OFF
57 W&H 16/26 REPS 2 SETS	**58** OFF	**59** GC ADD WEIGHT 12 REPS 2 SETS	**60** OFF	**61** W&H 18/28 REPS 2 SETS	**62** OFF	**63** GC 12 REPS 2 SETS
64 OFF	**65** W&H 18/28 REPS 2 SETS	**66** OFF	**67** W&H 20/30 REPS 2 SETS	**68** OFF	**69** GC 14 REPS 2 SETS	**70** OFF
71 W&H 12/22 REPS 3 SETS	**72** W&H 12/22 REPS 3 SETS	**73** OFF	**74** GC 14 REPS 2 SETS	**75** OFF	**76** W&H 14/24 REPS 3 SETS	**77** W&H 14/24 REPS 3 SETS
78 OFF	**79** GC 16 REPS 2 SETS	**80** OFF	**81** W&H 16/26 REPS 3 SETS	**82** W&H 16/26 REPS 3 SETS	**83** OFF	**84** GC 16 REPS 2 SETS
85 OFF	**86** W&H 18/28 REPS 2 SETS	**87** W&H 18/28 REPS 2 SETS	**88** OFF	**89** GC 18 REPS 2 SETS	**90** W&H 20/30 REPS 2 SETS	**91** GC 20 REPS 2 SETS

little roll of fat at the top of each thigh? Do you sag at the bottom of the fanny? Do your breasts droop? If you're really honest with yourself about the way you look in the mirror, you won't need a tape measure to tell you where the problems are. They're right there where you've been hiding them from yourself all this time.

Record your measurements and your visual impressions. Write a critique of yourself ("roll of fat around the waist," "flab on bottom of upper arm," etcetera), then make a list of all the trouble spots you've identified. Make the list as specific as you can: "upper hips" and "lower abdominals," instead of just "hips" and "waist." Find the exercises that work these specific areas. Plug them into your overall program. Make up the individual exercise periods with them. That's how you do specific work on specific areas that need attention. In a few minutes, we'll show you exactly how to make up a program, and we'll give you a program designed for those problem areas that most affect women.

Opposite is a chart for a 90-day program, aimed at general conditioning and sculpting. The specific area of specialization toward the end of the program is the waist and hips. The program consists of four basic Routines, with combinations of all four: (1) Stretching and Limbering (S & L), (2) General Conditioning (GC), (3) Waist and Hips (W & H), and (4) Specialized Bodysculpting. It's as simple as can be, now that we've got everything pinned down. Let's get right to it.

Look over the chart, and then refer to the succeeding pages for a detailed explanation of the abbreviations used in the chart, the exercise modules these abbreviations refer to, and the order in which the specific exercises should be done.

At the end of the chapter, we've included a blank chart, so that you can work up a program that meets the particular needs indicated by your personal problem areas.

ROUTINE NUMBER ONE: STRETCHING AND LIMBERING

Look back at the section at the beginning of Chapter Four. Read the descriptions of the Karate stretching and limbering exercises again. Now do the following:

NAME OF STRETCHING EXERCISE	NUMBER OF REPETITIONS
NECK (1), (2) and (3)	10 each
SHOULDERS (1) and (2)	10 each
UPPER BACK	10
CHEST	10
LOWER BACK	10
SIDES	10
ABDOMEN	10 with each leg
HIPS	10
BACKS OF THE KNEES	10 with each leg
LEGS	10

That's the first Routine, and you will do it for the first three workouts. Do 10 reps for each one for the first workout, 12 reps for each on the second workout, and 15 reps for each on the third workout.

This is a sort of "break-in" routine, that will give you the necessary suppleness to begin the next phase without pulling anything and causing minor aches. Do the routine for three days in a row, then rest for a day before beginning the next routine.

REMEMBER: you should always do some stretching and limbering before a workout, even when you have progressed to a full exercise program. It is a good idea to continue to do the stretching and limbering routine before the workout but do only 5 reps for each exercise. That way, you'll be thoroughly warmed up each time, but you won't wear yourself out during the warmup.

So, workouts 1, 2, and 3 are the Stretching and Limbering routine. Rest a day, then start the General Conditioning routine for the 4th workout. Thereafter, you'll want to take a day off between workouts in order to allow your metabolism to catch up with the energy expended during the workouts. Don't work out every day once you've passed this first phase.

ROUTINE NUMBER TWO: GENERAL CONDITIONING

If you take one or more exercises from each of the seven modules listed in Chapter Four, you will have an excellent general conditioning routine. It is not necessary to do every exercise listed in each module. You'll want to work out large groups of muscles at first, and then specialize later. Begin the routine with the number of repetitions and sets listed below. Consult the chart for increases in reps, sets and weight during the 90-day period.

In the case of the Seated Twist exercise, don't worry about reps or sets, and simply do 5 minutes of twists during each workout. It will give you time to rest up from the more strenuous exercises.

ROUTINE NUMBER TWO: GENERAL CONDITIONING

EXERCISE	NUMBER OF REPS	NUMBER OF SETS
SITUPS	10	1
LEG RAISES	10	1
SIDE LEANS	10 to each side	1
GOOD MORNING EXERCISE	10	1
SQUATS (with weight if possible)	10	1
SEATED TWISTS	five minutes	1
CALF RAISES	10	1
PRONE PRESSES	10	1
CURLS	10	1
SHOULDER SHRUGS	10	1

As you can see, each one of these exercises works out a group of muscles, and will give you general conditioning and general shaping as well. It is the basic routine we recommend, and it is the core of any genuine conditioning program.

If you are on schedule, you are in the 5th week of the program, and it is time to add another kind of routine to the one for general conditioning. In short, it's time to get down to the serious business of Bodysculpture. But let's take stock of ourselves first.

You've gone through 25 days of stretching, limbering and general conditioning. You should be able to tell a real difference by now. Your body should be generally leaner, more muscular, more toned-up and trimmed down if (and only if!) you've been sticking to your diet too (more on that later).

Encouraged? You should be. Your clothes are looser, you move with more ease and grace, your friends, no doubt, are telling you how fabulous you look. So let's take the next step. Whatever the problem, we have an exercise for it. We've been going now for a month. We have two more to go. Now comes the time for real self-appraisal.

Take another look in your mirror. Then get out the tape measure again. Take your measurements now, twenty-five days and many hours of exercise after the first time you measured. Some of the problem spots may have disappeared and others may be on their way out. Take your measurements carefully, and compare them with the first entry. You can tell right away where you've been making progress and where you still have work to do.

If you're like the majority of women, your remaining problem areas will be two: waist and hips. I'd guess that 80 percent of women who are (or think they are) overweight have problems chiefly in these two areas. Upper arms, thighs, calves, and backs seem to respond quickly enough to exercise. The general conditioning routine is usually enough to bring these areas into line. But sometimes certain areas don't respond and need special attention. For Valerie, it's her lower calf and ankles. But since for most women the hips and waist are the problem areas, let's develop a routine concentrating on hips and waist. (If these are not *your* problem areas, you'll be able to develop your own routine by paying attention to how we construct this one.)

ROUTINE NUMBER THREE: WAIST AND HIP MODULES

Look back at the list of exercises again. Bulging belly and drooping fanny mean fat in the abdominals and in the lower hips. You are already doing situps and leg raises as part of the general conditioning routine. Now add front crunches and alternating leg raises. Sometimes the fat that sticks out in front is also filling in the abdominal region where it connects with the sides. Consequently, if that's the case, you should add side crunches to the routine.

How about the sagging fanny? There are no exercises in the general conditioning routine for this problem, are there? But wait, there are different positions for the knees when you are doing the squat. The squat works out the lower hips too. Okay, what else? Well, there are lunges, back leg extensions, and the excess baggage roll.

What have we found? The following: front crunches, side crunches, alternating leg raises, lunges, back leg extensions, and the excess baggage roll. Seven exercises for the belly and the sagging fanny. Since we take a day off between each workout, let's just add situps and leg raises to the routine. Let's add seated and leaning twists too. That takes care of all the waist exercises and all the hip exercises for the area that you want to work out. That makes ten exercises, not including squats with the knees in position so that the hips will be worked out. That's enough. Overdoing it is as bad as not doing it at all. Now how should the exercises be arranged for the workout routine? REMEMBER A RULE OF THUMB: always put one of the less strenuous exercises in the middle of the routine, so that you will have a chance to get your breath back before going on with the rest of the routine. So, here's our suggestion:

EXERCISE	NUMBER OF REPS	NUMBER OF SETS
SITUPS	20	2
FRONT CRUNCHES	10	2
SIDE CRUNCHES	10	2

EXERCISE	NUMBER OF REPS	NUMBER OF SETS
EXCESS BAGGAGE ROLL	five minutes	1
LEG RAISES	20	2
ALTERNATING LEG RAISES	20	2
SEATED TWISTS	ten minutes	1
LEANING TWISTS	five minutes	1
BACK LEG EXTENSIONS	20	2

Now, as you can see, there are some things to explain. By the time that you start on the hip and waist module, you should be doing at least 20 situps during each workout period. Also, by the time that you start the H and W module, you should be doing ten minutes of seated twists. Further, you can see that we've started off with two sets for all the exercises except the excess baggage roll, seated twists and leaning twists. The reason for this is simple: we are trying to burn off the fat, and multiple sets is the best way to do that. It's not really complicated, and the difference in the number of reps and sets is easy as long as you keep track of what you're doing. When you start the program, get yourself a small notebook and write down all the exercises you use. Make a space for notations about reps and sets. It'll help keep you from getting bored.

You'll also notice that we started with 10 reps on the crunches instead of twenty or more. That's because those crunches are hard to do, and you'll feel 10 reps of them before you would feel forty reps of regular garden-variety situps. You should still work up to higher and higher repetitions, however, at the rate of about two reps every other workout.

For the excess baggage roll and the two kinds of twists, you should aim for an eventual figure of 15 minutes for the twists and 10 to 15 minutes for the excess baggage roll, depending on how much time you have and want to devote. These are not particularly hard exercises, but act chiefly as massagers of the area that they affect.

ROUTINE NUMBER FOUR: SPECIALIZED BODYSCULPTING

Don't be surprised if you are genuinely sore after the first good specialization routine. You will have been working out muscles that have not been specifically worked out in the general conditioning routine, and your body will tell you about it. All to the good, since that is the surest indicator as to whether or not you are working out the correct muscle for the problem that you have. If it's your front lower abdominals that you are after, and the exercises that you do make the front lower abdominals sore, then you're on the mark.

What do you do if your problems haven't been completely licked at the end of the 90-day program? Hang in there! It took Valerie longer than 90 days to get rid of the inches and pounds that she had collected over 30 years of bodily misman-agement. The purpose of the 90-day program is to show you incontrovertible proof that you can make an incredible amount of progress in a short time.

The program is open-ended, as you may have realized by now. Keep concentrating on those problem areas, and they *will* yield. Keep up the general conditioning routine and you will *never* be out of shape again. Put it all together, and you will become the person that you want to be, and you will be that person from now on.

Let's say that you've responded well to the program and your problem areas are no longer problems. Now what? Do you keep on going forever, raising the number of reps and sets until you are doing 10,000 reps and five hundred sets of the calf raise, and eight hours a day of the seated twists?

Relax. Once you get where you want to go, then all you have to do is go on a maintenance routine. You do not have to go on forever. You do not have to keep on keeping on with increasing sets and reps. Some of you may be able to drop back to a lighter routine at the end of 90 days, and keep up the workouts just as they have been outlined, with lighter weight, fewer reps and fewer sets. Only you can decide what is the best maintenance routine for you. We can suggest several maintenance routines for you, but you must decide whether or not they suit the particular set of problems that you had before you went on the Bodysculpture program.

Also, a lot depends on how consistent you are in sticking with your diet. A great deal also depends on the stubbornness of the problem you're attacking. If the problem area has been a problem area all your life, you won't be able to solve the problem and go on a maintenance routine for that area right away. On the other hand, if the problem is a sagging tummy caused by having carried a baby for nine months, then the problem can be quickly taken care of and you will be able to go on a maintenance routine in a very short while.

It may sound absurdly simple, but the best maintenance routine is one that incorporates the exercises that you used to solve the problems in the first place. That's right. If your problem was hips and waist, then the best maintenance routine is one that is a lighter version of the one you devised as a special sculpting routine. If the problem area was the back, then use the module for the back that you incorporated into your Bodysculpture routine. The same goes for legs, arms, chest, and all the rest of the body areas.

If it took 20 reps and two sets for three months to get it off, you can probably drop back to 20 reps and one set, or maybe even 10 reps and one set, in order to maintain the figure you've achieved. You will be surprised at how little effort it takes to keep in shape and to keep your new shapeliness, once you've gotten things down to the right size.

As we've said, it seems absurdly simple, but that's the way it works. In fact, back in the chapter on Psyching Up, you'll remember that we said that there was no mystery here. Well, that's right. There's no mystery. And it is simple. Look back at all this, now that you've developed your routines and followed the program to success.

Here is the blank chart you'll need to work up your own personal program.

A SUMMARY

You're out of shape. You're overweight. Hell, you're fat! What to do? Three days of stretching and limbering. A day off. A workout using the general conditioning routine, then a day off between each workout. Increase the reps. Increase the number of sets. Increase the amount of weight. After about a month of general conditioning, add a routine that incorporates the exercise modules that specifically attack the area where you have problems. Alternate this routine with the general conditioning routine. Toward the end of the initial 90-day program, gradually do more and more of the specialized Bodysculpture routines and fewer of the general conditioning routines.

When the 90 days are over, take another look at yourself. If your problems are solved, go on a maintenance routine that is merely a lighter version of the routine you used to get where you are. If the problems persist, then concentrate on them and keep it up until they are solved, while in the meantime keeping on a maintenance routine for everything else. Stay on a diet and don't backslide.

You might also take a moment to realize how good you look and feel. Great, isn't it? Now let's talk about what you can eat while you are in the transition period.

CHAPTER 6

Diets: The Good, the Fad, and the Ugly

Let's decide what you should, should not and absolutely cannot eat if you want to sculpt your body properly.

First, a few words about the aesthetics of dieting. Yes, you read us right: "aesthetics." We think of food as a physical necessity. But for most of us, it's also a rewarding experience. It tastes good, smells good, looks good. It has texture, substance, visual appeal, even sound appeal. So dieting is often a miserable experience because it deprives us of this elemental pleasure.

If you don't believe it, think back on great meals you have eaten—the lingering lunch, the hearty five-course Greek feast, the Sunday brunch, the sinfully thick pizza. Food can be sensual, beautiful, satisfying, romantic, nostalgic, comforting. But when you diet, you voluntarily deprive yourself of this whole area of experience and consign yourself to days of endless salads, low-salt cottage cheese, diet soda, black coffee, and hardboiled eggs. And two weeks later, you shamelessly backslide to the sinful delights of ravioli and Big Macs and chocolate ice cream.

But with the new diet consciousness and general health consciousness across the United States, this is all beginning to change. Dieting is no longer the torturous, self-depriving exercise in total abstinence it once was. Diet foods, even the prepackaged ones, taste and look better. The latest thing in gourmet cooking is *cuisine minceur*—French *haute cuisine* stripped of its fattening creams, sauces, and calorie-laden desserts. There are diet cookbooks galore, and excellent spas with tempting dietetic meals. From coast to coast there are fine health food and vegetarian restaurants. There's never been a better time to diet. As for specifics . . .

GET READY FOR YOUR DIET

Getting psychologically geared up for your diet is, in a way, your hardest project. It helps to get yourself ready for the great event by clearing your cupboard and refrigerator. Give away or at least put out of arm's reach all the "fat foods" that have helped you accumulate all the unwanted pounds—the breads, pastas, candies, cookies, colas, potato chips that made you look as you do now. Eliminate junk foods and processed foods: refined flour and sugar, lard and saturated fats, packaged mixes, salt, syrup-packed fruits.

Next, go grocery shopping. (Go immediately after a meal or you will find yourself tempted to buy forbidden goodies.) Stock your shelves with the following things:

Herbs and spices
Vanilla flavoring
Cinnamon sticks and cloves
Salt substitute
Fresh lemons or lemon concentrate
Bottled mineral water and diet sodas
Plain yogurt and/or low-fat cottage cheese
Sugar substitutes (if you need them)
Raw honey and blackstrap molasses
Coffees and teas (especially herbal teas)
Potassium broth or low-salt vegetable broth
Vegetable and fruit juices (no salt or sugar added)
Vegetable or peanut oil for cooking
Melba toast
Plain wheat germ, bran or brewer's yeast
Megavitamin pills
Unsalted sunflower seed and soy nuts (for nibbling)

Skim milk
Raw vegetables, apples and tangerines for snacks

Before you restock your refrigerator, give it a thorough washing out with warm water and baking soda. The smell is wonderfully fresh and helps remove all the old food odors. Rearrange refrigerator, pantry, and cupboard shelves with all your new purchases. If you must keep non-diet food for your family, put it out of easy reach. Get used to a refrigerator full of fresh produce and yogurt and mineral water instead of junk foods. Start reeducating yourself and your family about what it means to be well fed, and you'll do yourself and them a great service.

MAKE YOUR DIET MEALS FUN

We've already said that often diets don't work because food is associated in our minds with aesthetic experience. You'll stay on the diet longer with less backsliding if you make your diet as painless as possible. Take a tip from restaurateurs who insist on beautifully served meals, attractive china and glassware, and immaculate table linens. Prepare and eat your diet meals with all the ceremony of a master chef.

Have fresh flowers in a low bowl, scented candles, china ashtrays, elegant placemats, fresh linen napkins, or colorful big paper ones. Put your favorite record on the stereo. Arrange everything on large, important-looking plates; then fill up the plates with bits of orange or lemon peel, sliced green peppers, onion rings, sprigs of watercress or parsley, a bunch of four green grapes. Splurge on some sparkling mineral water and serve it in chilled, stemmed glasses with a slice of lime or lemon.

Make large vegetable salads and make a production of tossing, serving and eating them. Stretch your fruit allowance into an important dessert by cutting up apples, melons, berries, and tangerines into bite-sized chunks. Make a ritual of after-dinner coffee: espresso, cinnamon coffee, Turkish coffee. Add a cinnamon stick or vanilla bean for more flavor and no calories or sweeten the Turkish coffee with artificial sweetener. Serve thin slices of lemon peel with espresso. In short, replace quantity and calories with quality and visual appeal, and your diet meal will provide you with a kind of satisfaction that the three Big Macs and shake never did.

AVOID THE CHEAP FOOD AND FAST FOOD MYTHS

The most popular myths going are that diet food is both expensive and hard to prepare—a challenge to Julia Child and tremendously time-consuming. False, on both counts. Let's look at each of the myths in turn.

First, the money. True, most diets, especially of the low-calorie, low-carbohydrate variety, rely heavily on meat and fresh produce. Both are expensive. No one will deny that fowl, fish, beef, veal, and liver are growing dearer every day. The same for fresh produce: the cost of a single ripe tomato or head of fresh Bibb lettuce is sometimes staggering. But consider what you are giving up: bread, pasta, rice, processed cereal, refined sugar, all frozen and prepared foods, pizza, bacon, sausage and other breakfast meats, hot dogs, hamburgers, and most condiments. The list seems endless, but this small sample should give you an idea of the money you will now have available to put into lean meats, fish and fowl, eggs, cottage cheese, yogurt and fresh fruits and vegetables. The only other items you really need to add are juices and diet soda or coffee and tea.

One of the tragic things about the way Americans eat is that we spend literally billions of dollars of grocery money per year on "cheap" food—bread, spaghetti, cookies, pies, hamburger and hot dog buns, and so on. We are under the misconception that eating well and healthfully is a luxury we just can't afford. In reality, it's quite the opposite. It's the junk food, the frozen TV dinners, the Twinkies and Moon Pies and potato chips and tacos that send the grocery bill soaring. Even those of us on the most modest incomes could afford to eat dietetically if only we were prepared to cut out all junk foods. Gloria Swanson and Willam Duffy, co-authors of *Sugar Blues*, said in an interview that their total monthly food bill is actually less than that of the average welfare family in New

York City. Yet both travel with specially prepared food and mineral water, and insist on organically grown produce and fresh meat. If they can do it, so can you. The investment is in both health and appearance. What more could you ask, since it's possible on your budget too?

The myth that diet food is inordinately difficult to prepare is also a misconception, fostered partly by the abundance of excellent diet recipes and cookbooks. Wherever we turn, there seems to be some new version of a diet mousse or pâté to tempt us.

This isn't intended to diminish the value of the diet cookbook writers. Quite the contrary—they've made it possible to give variety to rigid diets. For those of us who love to cook, it's fun to make an Atkins-type cheesecake from cottage cheese, a Michel Guérard *pot de crème* (40 calories), or a dessert souffle (20 calories). But if you are rushed in the evenings, you can have a simple tossed salad, a grilled meat or fish entree, a dessert of fresh fruit, and a small cup of strong espresso and feel no need for anything fancier. You can add a clear consomme, beef bouillon or juice for a first course, or make a simple diet dessert, but the formula is good enough to repeat week after week without boredom. Save the fancy diet dishes for dinner parties and weekends—your guests and family will love you for keeping the meal light.

So you see, it *is* possible to cook what you want and need without too much difficulty or expense. By cutting out junk and replacing it with wholesome food (which is really what "diet food" is), and by getting rid of the notion that the table must be heaped with dishes, you can go on a diet, stay on a diet, enjoy the diet, and probably save money to boot. Forget the myths of expense and difficulty. That's all they are: myths that reinforce your non-dieting state, like a lot of the other myths we are trying to dispel in this book.

TRY SOME LOW-CAL GOURMET TREATS

Let's say it's the weekend. You've got dinner guests coming. Or you'd like a special dinner-for-two without blowing your diet. Take a look at these twenty-five low-calorie main dishes and diet desserts and see how appetizing dieting can really be. All are "dietetic" in the sense of being relatively low-calorie; most are low-salt and sugar-free. All are easy to prepare and can be made to last two days if you don't mind leftovers. Here's the list:

- London broil or roast beef, topped with a mushroom-shallot-leek-and-herb sauce
- Thin medallions of veal, broiled with lemon and herbs
- Rock Cornish hen, brushed with tarragon, rosemary, and diet margarine, with lemon juice and brandy extract added at the last minute before serving
- A half dozen fresh oysters in season
- A huge, fresh shrimp salad with diet shrimp sauce
- Quail or pheasant, stuffed with chopped apple cubes, chopped parsley, celery, seedless white grapes, and two tablespoons of brown rice, served with cranberry-horseradish relish
- Scrambled eggs, topped with a spoonful of plain yogurt, chives, and a teaspoon of caviar, served in an eggshell
- Half a papaya or melon filled with six cold shrimp or with jellied consomme
- Thin-sliced roast beef with all the fat trimmed away, served with melon wedges and lemon slices
- Leg of veal, roasted in cinnamon and lemon
- Filet of sole with dill sauce
- Tuna casserole with a spinach/mushroom/bean sprout base instead of pasta or noodles
- Julienne of turkey in aspic, served with cold white asparagus tips
- Spinach salad with crumbled bacon bits, red onion, mushroom, and bits of beef or Swiss cheese and hardboiled egg
- Eggplant "caviar" layered with cooked ground beef
- Broiled flank steak, marinated in soy sauce and ginger
- *Poule au pot* with fresh vegetables on the side
- Striped bass cooked in fennel and seaweed, served hot or cold
- Fresh bay scallops, served with endive and apple salad
- Veal chop (or lamb chop) *en casserole* with truffles
- Baked salmon with herbs
- Baked rainbow trout, cooked in safflower oil with herbs
- Grilled calves' liver topped with fresh mushrooms
- *Coq au vin* (dietetic sauce made with unsalted tomato juice, brandy extract, bacon bits, fresh onions, mushrooms, tomatoes and carrots, and thickened with two tablespoons of soy flour)

- Crepes made with a cottage cheese base and stuffed with spinach, diced chicken, mushrooms, or beef (base is a cup of cottage cheese, 1 egg, 2 small packets of artificial sweetener, 1 tablespoon cornstarch for thickening)

Now for dessert. These few suggestions should start you to thinking of the endless possibilities:

- Dessert souffle made of orange zest, four eggs (separated), grated orange rind and artificial sweetener
- Dietetic *pots de crème* (coffee or lemon)
- Meringue shell filled with fresh berries or diet preserves and a teaspoon of Reddi-whip
- Fresh pear halves poached in lemon juice, cinnamon and artificial sweetener
- Baked grapefruit sprinkled with cinnamon and artificial sweetener
- Honeydew melon boat filled with blueberries and strawberries
- Cold lemon souffle made with skim milk
- Ricotta or cottage cheese pie (Atkins recipe) with diet preserves or fresh strawberries
- Frozen "fake coffee" ice cream

TRY *NOT* EATING THREE MEALS A DAY

As for the other two customary meals a day (we've already taken care of dinner for you), rethink them. Who besides your mother and your grade-school nutrition teacher said you need a big breakfast or a huge lunch? You may do best with four or five small meals (or snacks) a day, spaced at intervals of three or four hours apart. Try it. Current diet research indicates that nibbling or snacking rather than eating a full meal results in less weight gain. Part of it is the reeducation of your own eating patterns. Try making a full four- or five-course meal a rare thing, reserved for festive occasions, and see how your weight pattern is affected.

Educate your thinking, too, about what constitutes food for a certain meal. Take breakfast, for instance. Why do you need eggs *and* a breakfast meat *and* toast (and possibly cereal) with butter and preserves and juice or fruit and coffee? Any one or two of these in combination will make a satisfying breakfast. You might enjoy one of these diet breakfasts: an egg with cottage cheese; plain yogurt topped with wheat germ and honey; fruit or juice with a mix of wheat germ, honey, sunflower and sesame or pumpkin seeds on the side—all served with drip grind, instant decaffeinated coffee or herbal tea.

Be daring and invent your own combinations: fish or meat with a slice of melba toast, the egg and caviar dish (see previous section), diet crepes filled with chopped chicken or eggs. Keep it light though nutritious, and you'll have the energy of a big breakfast without the bloated feeling.

Lunch can be as simple as a big glass of freshly made vegetable juice (carrots, celery, watercress, parsley, and cucumber) with unsalted seeds and a Frogurt cone on the side. A large salad is available at nearly all restaurants, and so are omelettes and plain grilled meats. At worst, you can get a roast beef sandwich and leave the bread and sandwich dressing on the plate. If you begin to lag at three or four o'clock in the afternoon, have a small can of vegetable or fruit juice or a cup of lemon tea with a spoonful of honey.

Another delicious combination is a bit of leftover coffee from the morning pot (which you have by now chilled in the refrigerator), mixed half-and-half with skim milk, a dash of vanilla, a sprinkling of cinnamon and some artificial sweetener—a sort of iced *café au lait*, delicious tasting, and you can heat it in the winter for a wonderful, rich-tasting diet drink.

As you might guess from reading this, Valerie's metabolism adjusts best to several small snacks rather than to the more customary large meals. You have to experiment with your own chemistry to see what works best for you. Valerie also finds she does better with moderately big lunches rather than dinners, so she tries to keep night dining simple and early. If we must eat late, we try never to order a full meal, but instead feast on salad and an appetizer. You may thrive on a moderately big breakfast and a lighter lunch with no dinner at all. Or you may want to begin the day with a breakfast drink of eggs, honey, protein powder, juice and skim milk, eat a moderately heavy lunch, then eat lightly at night. Some "night people" find they do best with a heavy dinner and little else all day. Try some experimentation. You may be delighted at the results.

AVOID FAD DIETS

How about the popular diets that everybody is talking (and sometimes complaining) about? What makes a good diet or a bad diet? If it's possible to eat as well as we've seen on the last few pages, why the necessity to go on a "crash" diet? What are the most popular diets and what makes them tick? Here's a quick, easy guide through the perils of the fad diet jungle.

The Atkins Diet

This controversial diet is a complicated version of the standard high-protein, low-carbohydrate diet. It is very complicated because it is built on modules of days (days 1–4, for example, are under different rules than days 5–9 when you begin to add a few carbohydrates on the approved list). It is considered potentially dangerous, according to the *Medical Letter of Drugs and Therapeutics*, especially to people with undiagnosed kidney disease, because the initial phase of the diet is not low-carbohydrate but *zero* carbohydrate. Furthermore, the unrestricted quantities of protein and fat can actually cause you to gain weight. The weight loss is often illusory. You may lose rapidly in the first week, but as soon as carbohydrates are added back to the diet, the weight comes right back in the form of regained water.

The object of the Atkins diet is to achieve the state of *ketosis*, which has possible unpleasant effects including accelerated and irregular pulse, extreme fatigue and hyperactivity, nausea, twitching of the limbs, calcium depletion, and kidney, bladder and colon trouble. Dr. Atkins himself in his 1973 testimony before the Senate Select Committee on Nutrition and Human Needs refers to the AMA criticism of keeping patients in a prolonged state of ketosis, but counters the attack by pointing out the difference between ketosis and the pathological state of ketoacidosis. Although some doctors may recommend a modified form of the diet for hypoglycemic patients, you should be thoroughly tested and checked out by a reputable physician before trying this or any diet.

The Stillman Diet

There are several versions of this diet, the two most popular and most publicized being the "quick-inches-off" diet and the "quick-weight-loss" diet. The first is the reverse of Atkins': it is a high-carbohydrate, low-protein program, which Stillman claimed would help you spot-reduce in exactly the places where you most needed it.

The second version is high-protein, low-carbohydrate, and is very close to Atkins'. Here, too, you don't count calories: you eat all the eggs, meat, poultry, fish, and seafood that you want, provided you also drink eight glasses of water a day and avoid all dairy foods except cottage cheese. The difficulty with the diet, aside from its dangers, is that diet alone cannot help you spot-reduce. The type of food eaten has no connection to the places where a loss in inches occurs. Only a program such as Bodysculpture can do that.

The Weight Watchers Diet Plan

This plan was developed by Jean Nidetch, who also developed the Diet Workshops and TOPS organization as supportive aids for the would-be loser. It is nutritionally balanced, since it involves weighing portions of food and eating, basically, a rather ordinary diet with small amounts of everything: breads, starches, even desserts. Weight Watchers also packages and distributes calorie-controlled frozen meals: luncheons, dinners, even light suppers and snacks. Many of the meals, in fact, seem too heavy on starches and sauces to be potential reducing diets for very long.

Reactions to the diet vary. Many find the workshops and weekly meetings supportive and helpful; others are bored or insulted by the evangelical tone. You can probably guess your own reactions to both the diet and the group sessions better than anyone else. Certainly the diet is not dangerous. It is balanced and nutritionally sound, and the calorie-controlled portions take all the guesswork out of meal preparation. It's all a matter of personal preference, but beware those heavy sauces and pastas.

The Magic Mayo Diet

This one is something like the Holy Roman Empire, which at the end was neither holy, Roman nor an empire. This diet is certainly not magic and it is in no way connected with the famous Mayo Clinic, according to Dr. Judith S. Stern (writing in *Vogue Beauty and Health Guide*, 1975–76). The trick here is a half grapefruit or a glass of grapefruit juice with every meal. Otherwise, it allows all the meat, fish and eggs you can eat, in addition to restricted quantities of sugar and starches. The grapefruit supposedly acts as a catalyst to aid in the digestion of fats—hence the "magic" epithet. Whether or not grapefruit has special fat-burning properties is a matter of some controversy between medical experts and diet faddists. Whatever the outcome of the debate, this diet is simply another high-fat, high-protein, low-carbohydrate diet and falls under the same scrutiny as Atkins and Stillman on that account.

Fasting

This is one of the latest fads and is currently being touted as the "ultimate diet." Indeed! Certainly it might well become *your* ultimate diet if you undertake it for too long a time. The strictness of such diets varies. Some permit only water, others allow absolutely nothing to pass the dieter's lips. Proponents not only claim miraculous losses of up to a pound a day; they also claim that it eliminates poisons from your body, promotes spiritual health, and gives you wonderful new insights into good, evil, freedom, and immortality. Perhaps. But it also gives you symptoms of dehydration and ketosis, plus dangerous loss of muscle tissue and important minerals, most notably potassium, calcium, and magnesium.

If you want to try a semi-fasting liquid diet, such as the famous Greenhouse or *Bazaar* three-day liquid diets, check with your doctor first. He can tell you if there are any special dangers involved, given your particular physical condition. The *Bazaar* three-day liquid diet is useful if you are retaining water. It consists of unsalted, natural vegetable and grapefruit juices, plain yogurt, and skim milk, taken in six small servings a day. The Greenhouse plan allows for natural juices, almond milk, and unsalted pine nuts or sunflower seeds for bulk. Both allow the water loss of fasting without the other ill side effects. But, we repeat: they should be followed only with the permission and supervision of your doctor.

The most popular fasting diet as we go to press is the liquid protein fast, developed by Drs. George Blackburn of Harvard, George Cahill of Jester Clinic, and Victor Vertes of Case Western Reserve University. Initially it was endorsed by the AMA's Dr. Philip White, head of the AMA Council on Food and Nutrition. The only "foods" allowed on this diet are vitamin pills and 300 to 500 calories' worth of a dark protein extract containing amino acids and glycogen. The diet is said to avoid protein tissue loss—a difficulty with most low-carbohydrate diets—and to concentrate on fat loss.

The diet is described in detail in Dr. Robert Linn's *The Last Chance Diet*. (Dr. Linn, a practicing physician in Pennsylvania, was among the first to put Drs. Cahill's and Blackburn's work into practice. Publisher Lyle Stuart lost 83 pounds in 120 days on a protein-sparing fast under his supervision.) The diet's advantages are obvious: it removes the element of choice and makes it possible for the dieter to live literally for weeks without making any choices related to food at all. But the diet has come under scrutiny. FDA Commissioner Donald Kennedy stated in November of 1977 that government health authorities suspect the diet as a contributing factor in the sudden deaths by heart attack of ten women under age 45. Whatever the validity of this claim, it is a diet to be used *only* under medical supervision. Effective, yes: potentially dangerous—perhaps. Only time can give us the answer on this one.

Liquid Diets Based on Diet Drinks

We are all familiar with the famous Metrecal and Slender plans, as well as other liquid diets. They were among the first special diet foods or drinks to make their appearance in diet-obsessed America. We hear less about them nowadays, whether due to the boredom of the diets or the new sensitivities of dieters' palates, it's hard to tell. Certainly, the popularity of the other, more interesting diets and the glut of diet cookbooks on the market has done much to eclipse the diet drinks. No doubt about it. They are dull, and because they are dull, the temptation is to go off them almost at once.

On the plus side, they are nutritionally balanced, calorie-controlled, easy to shop for and prepare (just pop the top), and can be heated, iced, spiced, or frozen for variety. They are often useful to start a diet. They help break the meal routines that we get ourselves into when we're eating too well. And they will peel off an unwanted two or three pounds quickly. Personally, four or five days seems to be our limit, and we suspect it's yours too. Experiment with your own psyche and metabolism. If you stay on the diet drinks for any length of time, you will need to add bulk in the form of salad greens, nuts or seeds, or bran tablets. But you may find the drinks the perfect diet for you, and if so, drink away with our blessings.

The Lecithin, B_6, Vinegar and Kelp Diet

This one was developed by Mary Ann Crenshaw. Basically, it's a simple low-calorie diet which also calls for two tablespoons of lecithin per day, B_6 tablets, a teaspoon of apple cider vinegar, and six kelp tablets after each meal. The rationale is that lecithin emulsifies the fat, B_6 metabolizes it, while vinegar restores your potassium balance and kelp supplies iodine to make the thyroid gland speed up your metabolism.

The diet is fairly well-balanced nutritionally, and the vitamins and minerals are safe enough if not used to excess. Be careful, however, of overdosing on lecithin—it is present in many foods in the natural state. We both found by personal experience that an excess can deplete the body's potassium supplies and you may experience dizziness, ringing in the ears, jitteriness, involuntary muscular twitchings, and a host of other ailments. Probably your best bet is to take the capsules that were a commercial spinoff of the diet's success, and avoid the massive dosage recommended by the diet's advocates.

Vegetarian, Organic and Macrobiotic Diets

These diets vary greatly, depending on which version you adopt and how you supplement it with vitamins and minerals. Macrobiotic diets, for example, vary from well-balanced low-calorie diets to the "ultimate" macrobiotic diet, which consists only of brown rice.

Most "organic" and health food diets, if they are really dietetic, are simply low-calorie or calorie-controlled diets with the emphasis on natural foods (no additives or preservatives), organically grown vegetables, and fertile eggs. (Careful with the organic produce. Unless it is washed thoroughly and cooked, the various microbes in the natural compost used for growing may cause more trouble than the missing preservatives.)

Organic grains and raw honey are fine, as are plain or naturally flavored yogurts and cottage cheeses. But don't be misled by confusing "organic" or "natural" with dietetic. The two are not synonymous. In fact, many foods advertised as natural are actually quite high in calories—for example, organic cereals such as sweetened granola, organic peanut butter or whole-grain flours, pastas, and noodles. *Repeat:* "organic" and "natural" do not necessarily mean dietetic or nutritious. The terms simply mean that the products were grown without chemical fertilizers and sometimes without insecticides.

Vegetarian diets are usually based on soybeans, beans, rice, and perhaps dairy foods and eggs. Many of these are high in fiber and low in cholesterol, but also are high in calories and vegetable fats as well as carbohydrates. It is virtually impossible to remain on a low-carbohydrate vegetarian diet because of the need for beans and legumes for supplements. Then, too, vegetable protein is not really sufficient. One needs the balance of at least small amounts of animal matter to allow for the enzymes necessary for the digestion of the vegetable protein. It is best to supplement with at least some fowl and fish dishes to allow for the essential digestive ingredients.

There are many other diets, of course, some of which were past fads, others of which are the up-and-coming thing. To the list above you can add your own: the ice cream diet, the bananas-only diet, the Drinking Man's Diet (a notorious failure, since alcohol is high in calories), the snacker's diet, the hamburger diet, and now the Junk Food Diet. Most have one difficulty in common: nutritional imbalance, resulting from overemphasis of one food to the exclusion of others. Many stress water loss rather than real weight loss. And some capitalize on the common myth that certain foods allow you to lose weight segmentally. We repeat: no way. Only a systematic exercise routine can shape the parts of your body as you wish. Diet will result in an overall weight loss; it's then up to you to sculpture that loss in the most pleasing way.

TRY THIS RECOMMENDED DIET

What are some good diets to try with all this mishmash of bad ones? The best are the simple tried-and-true low-calorie ones: the famous *Bazaar* ten-day diet, the American Heart Association diet, or almost any good, standard low-calorie diet prescribed by your doctor and sanctioned by legitimate nutrition authorities. If you would like a quick two-week regimen to get you started, try this one after checking first with your doctor:

DAYS 1–3

BREAKFAST: Tea or coffee with artificial sweetener
Unsweetened grapefruit juice or unsalted tomato or V-8 juice
Hardboiled egg or 4 oz. low-salt cottage cheese

LUNCH: Tossed green salad with oil and vinegar dressing
4 oz. cottage cheese or 4 oz. yogurt (plain)
Coffee, tea or diet soda

DINNER: 4 oz. cottage cheese, yogurt or skim milk
Small apple, tangerine, or 10 white grapes
Coffee, tea or diet soda

DAYS 4–14

BREAKFAST: Hardboiled egg or 4 oz. cottage cheese with plain wheat germ or bran sprinkled on top
Juice (no salt or sugar added)
Coffee or tea

LUNCH: Broiled chicken or fish, lean roast beef (with fat trimmed away), or omelette (plain or herbed)
Large vegetable salad with oil and vinegar dressing
Coffee, tea or diet soda

DINNER: Large vegetable salad or tray of *crudités*
4 oz. cottage cheese or plain yogurt
1 oz. unsalted sunflower or pumpkin seeds
1 small apple, tangerine, 2 oz. white grapes or berries

ALLOWABLE SNACKS: Assorted *crudités* (sliced carrots, celery, zucchini, cherry tomatoes, mushrooms, pepper strips, cucumber wedges, cauliflower buds, radishes, and red cabbage)

A handful of sunflower, pumpkin or sesame seeds or soy nuts (unsalted)
A slice or two of dried fruit or 1 oz. raisins

NOTE: The diet's effectiveness will be increased if on day 7 and day 11 you return to the days 1–3 formula.

If you add to this regimen only the following ingredients, you could stay on it indefinitely:

Fats—a teaspoon of safflower oil or peanut oil for cooking; a pat of diet margarine

Carbohydrates—a few extra teaspoons of honey, more fruit, fresh-squeezed orange juice or apple juice; extra dried fruit or raisins

Grains and breads—unprocessed bran, unsweetened wheat germ, unsweetened granola, unsalted pumpernickel Melba toast, unsalted pumpkin seeds and soy nuts

Dairy products—unsalted cheese, ricotta cheese, plain yogurt or Frogurt, more skim milk

Additives—a tablespoon of brewer's yeast and a tablespoon of lecithin granules stirred into yogurt or juice

As for the number of calories you should consume per day, that is an individual matter and varies radically from person to person. In fact, it may even vary with different periods in your life, depending on your age, general physical condition, activity, stress, and so on. You will need to experiment here. If the portions prescribed add up to, say, 1000 calories a day and you are not losing weight, reduce the portions by a third and see what happens. Or eliminate one or two foods with higher caloric content and test the results.

Remember, there's no law that says you must eat "normal" sized portions of everything. You can gain weight on an eight-ounce carton of yogurt a day, but thrive on a half-carton *and* lose weight at the same time. Experiment, too, with changing the time of your largest meal(s). Rather than cutting out all foods but a few and living exclusively on them, as fad diets urge you to do, cut the size of the portions until you begin to lose. Later, when you go on a "maintenance" diet, you can begin to add size to the servings again.

To help you along, here is a list of the foods that you should be able to eat on a daily basis. Some items are higher in calories than others, so be careful in your calorie count. It is a balanced list, and when you eat, take small portions of everything. If you don't, your tape measure (and scales) will let you know in a hurry that you've slipped.

VEGETABLES

Spinach	Cauliflower
Bean sprouts, alfalfa sprouts	Carrots
Artichokes	Radishes
Green pea pods	Red cabbage
Brussels sprouts	Tomatoes
Water chestnuts	Green peppers
Tofu (Oriental bean curd)	Green onions
Asparagus	Squash
Lettuce	Pumpkin
Endive	Zucchini
Chicory	Leeks
Parsley	Watercress
Broccoli	Green beans

FLAVORINGS

Spices and herbs	Salt substitute
Raw honey	Black pepper
Lemon	Safflower or peanut oil
Cider vinegar	

MEATS, FISH AND FOWL

Lean, thin sliced beef (broiled or roasted, with the fat removed)
Chicken, turkey, Cornish hen, capon, squab, pheasant (all boned and skinned)
Fresh, unbreaded fish, bluepoint oysters, crab claws, frog legs, boiled shrimp, broiled veal or calves' liver

FRUITS (fresh or water-packed)

Melon (honeydew, cantaloupe, or African)	Grapefruit
Pineapple	White seedless grapes
Apples	Strawberries
Tangerines	Raspberries
Nectarines	Blueberries

JUICES AND SOUPS
Unsweetened grapefruit, apple, or cranberry juice
Fresh vegetable juice (celery, carrot, parsley, cucumber)
Low-salt consomme or bouillon
Potassium broth

OTHER LIQUIDS
Diet sodas
Plain soda water
Mineral water
Black coffee
Iced or hot tea
Espresso

EGGS AND DAIRY PRODUCTS
Skim milk
Eggs (hardboiled or poached)
Ricotta cheese, farmer's cheese, or low-fat cottage cheese
Low-fat plain or vanilla-flavored yogurt

GRAIN OR NUTS
Melba toast (unsalted)
Wheat germ (unsweetened)
Bran (unsweetened)
Sunflower, sesame, or pumpkin seeds (unsalted)
Soy and pine nuts (unsalted)
Unsweetened granola

WATCH FOR WATER RETENTION PROBLEMS

A word of caution about liquids. Oftentimes a weight problem goes hand-in-hand with a water retention problem. The fluid retention can range from mild to severe—up to six pounds a day in difficult cases. If you find your weight fluctuating wildly with gains of over a pound in twenty-four hours, fluid retention is probably the culprit. This is *not* a problem that you can solve for yourself. You need the assistance of a doctor to help you decide if fluid retention is involved in your weight problem. If it is, medication or a low-salt diet is often prescribed to correct the condition. If the problem is mild, you can help yourself by avoiding orange juice, beans, peas, bananas, and highly salted and/or spiced dishes.

Stay instead with melon, grapefruit (and grapefruit juice) or unsalted tomato juice, white grapes, fresh mixed vegetable juice, skim milk, plain yogurt, asparagus, apples, pumpkins, cabbage, watercress, radishes, lettuce, cumin and sage. All these foods have helpful diuretic properties, as do some teas: cornsilk, horsetail, rosehip, and many other herbals. Coffee will act as a mild diuretic if taken in small quantities, but be careful—too much can backfire. And diet sodas can help with fluid retention problems if drunk in moderation. If you drink them to excess, they will cause bloating. Your best bet as drinks go is bottled mineral water, sipped slowly through a straw. Perrier water, either straight from the bottle or in a glass with a sliver of lime on top, is a delicious and very In drink right now. It's lovely to look at and a good diuretic besides.

If you wish, you might ask your doctor's advice about using a salt substitute in place of regular table salt. Many of these substitutes are also high in potassium—an added bonus for dieters. Most of us could cut down on the amount of salt we now use: we all oversalt our food and oversugar our drinks. Unsalted vegetable juices and salads are delicious and delicately flavored. All it takes is a bit of time to become accustomed to the saltless taste (you will be surprised how much salt is already in the food you eat). But we repeat: whatever you do, don't take medicinal diuretics without medical advice.

"PSYCH" YOURSELF INTO YOUR DIET

Dieting, as we pointed out earlier, is largely a matter of aesthetics. It is also a matter of your own psychology. You can psych yourself into (and, alas, out of) a diet. It's all a matter of where your head is.

Part of the psychology of dieting is putting yourself into a frame of mind where your attention is focused less on immediate gratification than on the rewards of looking and feeling better. In other words, the psychological gimmick is the denial of immediate self-gratification for the sake of another, delayed reward. That's a very adult, intellectual form of gratification, much more sophisticated than the instant rewards that most of us learned to expect as we grew up—candy *now*, an ice-cream cone *today*.

Which all means that in order to diet and follow the Bodysculpture program that we outline here, you must become more the adult than the child. You must learn to say "no" to yourself without becoming the punishing parent and invoking feelings of self-pity or rebelliousness ("Why should I have to give up my chocolate ice cream?").

It helps to find your own psychological gimmick. One that worked for Valerie when she was very heavy was two pictures pasted on the refrigerator door. One picture was a lean, bikini-clad model on a sandy beach. The other was Valerie at her fattest in a Chubby Juniors dress from Lane Bryant.

A full-length mirror somewhere near the kitchen helps, as does a pair of scales or a tape measure. So does stripping the refrigerator and kitchen cabinets of fat-making foods. Throw them away if necessary. Make snacking hard on yourself. Raw vegetables, tiny chunks of raw fruit, a bit of wheat germ or bran or a wedge of low-salt cheese—these should be the only handy between-meals food in your kitchen.

It also helps to keep a "diet diary." In a small notebook, record everything you have eaten during the day, the amount, the time, the place, and your mood when you ate. Figure the total calorie count at the end of the day. It's a revealing exercise to learn, not just how much you ate in terms of calories, but also when and where and what you were feeling when you ate. You may nibble while you cook dinner, snack at parties, nosh at your desk. Or you may be a secret night eater who raids the fridge when the family is in bed. Whatever the pattern, the diet diary will let you see and correct it.

Finally, while the old "think-yourself-thin" ploy is at best a hoax, you *can* help psych yourself into a thin frame of mind. Learn to eat like a thin person—slowly, in a relaxed manner, leaving some food on the plate at the end of each meal. As you eat, imagine yourself as a thin person—the person you will in fact be at the end of your program. Now imagine that woman eating and drinking—small amounts, small bites, tiny sips of everything, with long pauses for talk and listening and looking. If you hold this image in your mind each time you sit down at the table, you will soon identify with this "thin person" and her eating habits. Try it. It's a marvelous psyching-up device to see you through the rough days of your diet.

TRY TO MAINTAIN YOUR DIET WHEN YOU GO OUT

Now the last (or next-to-last) hurdle: what do you eat when you go out? That's a bad one, because the pressure is on you to eat, especially if the menu is good and your companion wants the satisfaction of having wined and dined you in grand style. Remember: he may enjoy seeing you tie into all that food, but he'll be watching the other women at the beach tomorrow.

Here are some suggestions for different types of restaurants and for the foods they typically serve. Remember also: you don't have to eat everything on your plate.

AVERAGE AMERICAN STEAK HOUSE OR SEAFOOD RESTAURANT
Large salad, omelette, lean broiled meat or fish, boiled vegetables (including asparagus or artichokes), plain scrambled or boiled eggs, "diet plate" of lean hamburger, cottage cheese, and a salad

FRENCH RESTAURANT
Filet of sole, omelette *fines herbes*, mussels *rémoulade*, *escargots* or bluepoints, *paupiette de veau*, bouillabaisse, poached sea bass, trout, bay scallops, small *tournedos* of beef

GREEK RESTAURANT
Greek salad (plain or horiatky-style; leave the olives and anchovies

on the plate), gyros, roast lamb or shish kebab, *dolmades*, spinach-cheese pie, Greek or Turkish coffee with no sugar

ITALIAN RESTAURANT
Prosciutto and melon, vegetable plate (zucchini and eggplant without the rich sauce), a plain veal, chicken or fish dish, baked clams casino, broiled shrimp scampi, veal *paillard* or veal *rollatine*, chicken cacciatore, clams or mussels marinara. For dessert: a cup of espresso with a twist of lemon peel.

REEDUCATE YOURSELF ABOUT DIET

Finally, the hardest rule of all: learn to think of your diet not as a temporary period of deprivation but as a lifetime change in your eating habits. This may sound unthinkable to you, but let's consider it a moment. It took you your entire lifetime to accumulate all the extra pounds and inches you have acquired. Maybe you just gained them over the last few years, but you had the eating habits of a lifetime that set you up for the fall. You have a long life as a thin person ahead of you, and you may rest assured that losing all that weight will add years to your life.

But you have to learn to eat in a way suitable for your new body, for your new metabolism, your new level of physical activity and stamina, your new lighter body weight, and above all, your new body image. You may find that you simply can't eat a huge four- or five-course meal once you've lost the extra weight. Exercising increases your appetite temporarily, but eventually you will find yourself eating less. A full meal will become too much for you, but you will eat lightly with greater enjoyment than ever before once your weight has begun to stabilize.

Dieting as a way of life does not necessarily mean that you will never, ever in this mortal life taste another spoonful of ice cream or chocolate mousse or veal parmigiana. You will, of course. But you may not eat the entire serving. You may leave half, or split the order with a dieting companion. Or you may decide to indulge in one delicious entree and skip the appetizer and dessert. Or you may splurge and eat the forbidden goodie, then make up for it the next day by having only salad and tea for lunch.

Instant recap: however you adjust, if you are going about your diet the right way, you will compensate for the occasional binge and as a result your body weight will stabilize at or near the magic figure. You'll count calories, keep a diet diary, imagine the new thin you if these are the head tricks you need. You'll avoid fad diets and remember that you can't lose weight segmentally because of certain foods or supplements. Your eye and palate and head will be so attuned to your own dietary needs that you will know from a glance at the menu what you can order and what you can't. You'll keep a kitchen full of spices, fresh fruits and vegetables, lean meats, delicious coffees and teas, whole-grain natural cereals and low-calorie dressings and flavorings—no snack foods, junk food, or gooey desserts. When you reach that point, you will have made up your mind to make your diet a way of life, and you will have a healthier, leaner, more disciplined body to show for it.

CHAPTER 7

Fashion as Camouflage: What to Wear Until the New Shape Comes

The dream is that you walk into a party (office, restaurant, meeting, convention) and all eyes turn to you; everyone drops his or her fork (glass, conversation) and says, "What a beautiful woman just walked in!" But the reality is often very different. Every diet or exercise routine hits plateaus when a loss in pounds or inches seems impossible. If you're dealing in Bodysculpture rather than strict poundage loss, you're talking about the body segmentally. Different areas will respond to reshaping more dramatically than others. So you may look fine in some places and less good in others. One memorable plateau in Valerie's program: her waist was down to 23 inches but her legs and upper arms were still heavy. Thank heaven for long-sleeved T-shirts and pants. She lived in them that spring. Everyone thought that she looked wonderfully thin. In reality, she was living in a constant state of *camouflage* until the next few inches came off.

What do we mean by camouflage? Let's think about it this way. Some figure faults are genetic. You can't reshape your bone structure, grow shorter or taller, or change your body type. The length of the Achilles tendon (which connects the calf muscle to the bone at the heel) determines whether or not you get that lean, racehorse look of the top models. If you have a short Achilles tendon, you'll never have those marvelous bony ankles, no matter how much you diet and Bodysculpt and run and do high-repetition rise-on-toes exercises. If you have a long waist and torso in comparison to short legs, no amount of Bodysculpture is going to change that. Those are the givens, and you must learn to work within them.

Unfortunately, Valerie made the common mistake of expecting too much of her routine, and believed that once she got down to 125 pounds, she could wear anything she wanted. So she went from experimenting with nothing to experimenting with virtually everything. No fad or fashion was too wild for her to try: printed tights, short skirts, long skirts, hip-huggers, patched jeans, crocheted tops, lace-up boots.

She was still heavy, and that compounded the catastrophe. What you learn from costly errors such as these is that you cannot wear just anything you find in the stores. Instead of running out—pocketful of credit cards in hand—to embrace every new fad and fashion, you still have to pick and choose.

And this is how we came to develop the theory of fashion for women with figure faults that we call "fashion as camouflage." The purpose is to use clothes and accessories to deemphasize, disguise, even hide your worst points and play up the good ones. With careful shopping and fitting, heavy hips, legs, protruding tummy, thick midriff, and fat arms go into hiding and reappear only when the final reshaping effort has produced the maximum results possible.

Dress designer and fashion expert Edith Head once said that she could make any woman look ten years younger and ten pounds thinner with the proper choice of clothes. That's practicing fashion as camouflage, and that's exactly what we're recommending. You must learn what for you emphasizes slimness and height, and then buy those things, wear them in different combinations, and seldom deviate from them. But your dress never has to be dull. Here's a guide with simple, straightforward advice on what to wear to overcome specific problems.

FOR HEAVY LEGS

Valerie is the true expert in this problem, because it's her chief bugaboo. If we judge by the existing literature, no one else has the problem—at least not the readers of *Vogue, Mademoiselle, Glamour, Bazaar, Cosmopolitan*, or *Viva*. When advice to women with heavy legs is offered (which is rarely), the beleaguered fashion editor usually advises, "Cover them up." Fine, if you like to live in pants, more of a problem if you don't. So, let us offer hints on camouflage for legs. You can wear shoes, stockings, skirts, pants, but pay special attention to color, line, and design.

Rule One: Maintain an Unbroken Line

Whatever chops up a leg into different color areas shortens, thickens and visually breaks up the line of your legs. Don't be tempted by the gorgeous full-color spreads of models in purple satin ankle boots and red ribbed tights (worn with French leg warmers and satin garters). The models all have Veruschka-thin legs, so the purple and red scheme comes off much as it would on the proverbial beanstalk.

You must be more discriminating. If you are wearing a skirt, wear color-coordinated hose, shoes, and boots in black, charcoal gray, maroon, wine, dark brown, navy. Toning is the key: dark brown sheer hose and dark brown shoes with a chocolate colored skirt, black (or deep charcoal gray) with a pewter-gray or silver dress. Nothing is more flattering and leg-lengthening than a dark knee-length to mid-calf skirt, sheer opaque dark hose in the same tone, and matching shoes.

The formula need not be dull. The shoes can be two-tone (if subtle—no fuchsia and orange, please), the skirt can vary in style, material and cut, the hose *could* have a subtle rib or pattern in them. But toning-in is the key. The same tone or shades of the same color create the long unbroken line you're looking for.

The one exception: if you're wearing a white, beige or ivory skirt, choose a slightly darker shade of sheer hose (perhaps a coffee or light suntan shade) and tone in with an in-between shoe in beige, pale gray, or a black and beige Chanel-type sling. Tricky, but the slimming effect of the darker hose is worth it. No matter what the fashion magazines tell you, beware of flesh-toned hose if you have heavy legs. A shade or two darker gives the same effect and preserves the illusion of slimness.

Rule Two: Opaque Stockings Are Wrong for Heavy Legs

Particularly in warm weather, opaque hose look hot and add inches. Besides, they give a sort of stodgy, grandmotherly look. Certainly they call attention to the legs, and you, clever woman that you are, are trying to draw attention away from them. For everyday wear, the best bet is a semi-opaque or "sheer opaque" pantyhose (perhaps a control top, if you need it). Van Raalte and Hanes make some marvelous ones in shades that look good both summer and winter: coffee bean, jet, safari, rust, navy, and a subtle gray that looks smashing with most neutrals.

Rule Three: Very Sheer Hose Are Usually a Mistake for Everyday Wear

Save them for evenings and for evening clothes, such as chiffons or silks that simply will not take the weight of the semi-opaques. A very dark sheer often will work, but sheer lights in beige or rose-beige should be saved for wear under pants, long skirts, and dresses.

Rule Four: Avoid Ankle Straps, Mary Janes, Short Ankle-Length Boots (Except Under Pants), Anything with Short Socks, Needle-Thin Stiletto Heels, Lace-Up and Ankle-Tie Espadrilles (Except, Again, Under Pants), and Ghillies (Except as a Pants Shoe)

In general, a wide-throated high-vamp shoe in a dark color is best, with a high-medium straight, slender heel. Beware of heels that curve inward, such as the once-popular spool heel. On a woman with heavy legs, they look as if the leg crushed the heel by its sheer weight. On the other hand, you are not consigned to the plain dark pump forever. Sandals are all right (no ankle straps: keep the throat wide), low T-straps, moccasins, high narrow wedge heels, even lace-ups as pants shoes. Small to medium platforms are excellent because they give some counterbalancing weight to the foot and add height.

Rule Five: Boots Are a Godsend (Provided They Meet the Edge of Your Hem)

Stay away from the short cowboy style, the tight "grannies" or lace-ups, the huge Cossack type with the crushed ankle. Find a classic knee-high or over-the-knee slim straight-leg boot in dark leather with a highish, slender heel. They will probably cost you dearly, but they will be worn year in and year out, regardless of the whims of fashion. They are not only super camouflage for legs, they are also warm, practical, fashionable, and an excellent investment. Don't be afraid of the pull-on stretch boots. There are some attractive ones made, and because they hug the calf, they can shrink along with your new proportions. Keep the color dark, the styling classic, and the heels medium to high. The same applies for long stocking boots.

Rule Six: Avoid Horizontal Stripes, Loud or Large Patterns, Wild Prints Like Hot Sox (Unless You Use Them as Just a Flash of Color Under Pants or Jeans), Fish-Net Hose, Knee Socks with Shorts or Short Skirts

Contrary to most advice, also be wary of vertical stripes or ribbings. The vertical lines slim, yes. But if legs are too heavy, the pattern of the stripes will run askew all the time (especially over fat knees) and will result in a catastrophic look.

Rule Seven: Pants Are Not Always the Panacea for Heavy Legs That Everyone Thinks They Are

Yes to the above if your problem is confined to calves and ankles; no if thighs and hips are included. The best pants for disguising both heavy legs and a plump *derrière* are classically tailored, simple pants with a medium-wide waistband, no gathers in front (stitched or partly stitched pleats are all right), no back pockets or back detail of any sort, a slight flare at the leg and no cuffs—cuffs are a sure leg-shortener. If this sounds dull, look closely at the most expensive designer pants on the market—Calvin Klein, Ted Lapidus, Rafael, Saint Laurent—and you'll find that their pants all follow this same basic, classic pattern. Avoid hip-huggers until you reach an advanced state of *thin*, and then only for casual, resort, or evening wear; they cling to hips and thighs and emphasize whatever inches or remaining flab there is.

Rule Eight: Although Evening Pants Are Different, the Same Rules Apply That Apply for Daytime Pants

Evening pants will probably be pull-ons with an elasticized or drawstring waist, and will have slightly more flaring legs—evening pyjamas rather than tailored pants. One basic evening item that will get you through summer, winter, spring, fall and "transition" seasons is a pair of black silk or jersey pyjamas with slightly flared legs and a plain waistband. Team this classic with tank tops, tubes, even T-shirts and ethnic tops for informal evenings; with Lurex or jeweled tops, brocade, chiffon or silk for festive occasions. You could complement the pants for an evening of dancing with a glitter top and sweater, a filmy chiffon blouse, chiffon or gauze tunics, new or antique silk kimonos, and *crêpe de chine* or silk shirts knotted at the waist and dressed up with chains, pearls, or strands of turquoise and coral.

And don't neglect the long skirt for evening; it goes in and out of fashion, but at least one is a must. It's a super disguise for heavy legs and thighs, particularly if it is dark-colored, cut on the bias, and rather clingy—the St. Tropez swirl pattern with the long bias stripes does wonderful things for your hips. It should be at least ankle-length or longer. It can be a pleasant change from pants every night, and keeps your problem legs nicely hidden until you get the rest of your problems solved.

FOR HEAVY HIPS AND THIGHS

Rule One: The Slimming Effect of Pants Depends Strictly on the Cut

Look over the "heavy legs" section again. Pants work fine, but discretion is called for. Very subtle details in cut can make dramatic differences in the way the pants look on you. There is no substitute for time spent trying on, looking, rejecting, trying on again and altering, until exactly the right style and fit are found. The best bet is a well-fitted, beautifully tailored (never tight) pair of flared pants worn with highish heels or a medium platform or wedge for added height.

No matter how the fashion magazines tout the notion of the flat pants shoe or boots, all but very tall women should avoid them. The aim is to add to the illusion of height and slimness in any possible way. If you shy away from platforms or wedges, either for cosmetic or safety reasons, try a mocassin, city sandal, high-heeled pants boot, or a wide-throated ghillie with a three- to four-inch heel. If the pants are classic and tailored, these shoes will look casual and chic and still provide the necessary height to carry off the look.

Rule Two: Those with Heavy Hips Should Avoid Design Features That Call Attention to the Hips

If you're bottom-heavy, avoid horseshoe-stitched-bottom French jeans, back or hip pockets, trouser-pleated "baggies," cutesy back decor like decals or embroidery, back and front gathers, tight pants or skirts, short contrast-colored jackets, horizontal stripes, wide hip belts, shorts, hip-huggers, wild prints and huge flared legs. Don't be afraid of jeans if they're well-cut, tailored and pocketless; pants with small stitched darts or pleats at the waist; flowing jersey evening pants; or even pantsuits, provided the jacket is thigh-length at least.

Keep the lines simple and the interest focused at the waist, neck or on a colorful top or sweater. That way, pants can be a great lifesaver. For very, very heavy women, the best style is simple drawstring-waist pants in a soft fabric, or a jersey or wool pull-on with an elasticized waistband that can shrink with you.

Rule Three: If Your Fanny Is Too Heavy to Show, Then Cover It Up

A fine camouflage for heavy hips is the basic fanny coverup. This one can be a sleeveless vest, a slightly flared coat or tunic, a long cardigan or loose pullover sweater, a long loose hip-covering sweater (one of the John Ashpool-type patterned sweaters is a good investment), a loose blazer or shirtjacket, even a long shawl, scarf or poncho that reaches below the hipline.

Sweater coats, provided they are non-bulky, flat knits, are also excellent buys. The basic principle here is to keep it covered until you are ready to show it off. Scale your jackets, sweaters, and overblouses so that they cover this area. The key is the proportion: keep the lines straight, simple, and close to the body, cover the hips completely, create distractions with long scarves, beads, or striking pins, and several pounds are lost in silhouette.

A word about Big Tops, cardigan sweaters, vests, and blazers: keep them loose, in thin to clingy fabrics, and a bit on the fitted side, though not tight. A lighter one disguises and camouflages without adding the illusion of extra weight. Try to find something with a straighter, chemise-like line. A blazer that pinches in too far at the waist and flares out over the hips accentuates the heavy hip line and gives a matronly look. Often, a straight-cut shirtjacket is a better choice. Kimono tops that wrap and tie loosely are super. So are lightweight cardigans, especially in vertical stripes. So are lightweight shawls, ponchos, pullover sweaters, tunics, and overblouses.

Rule Four: You Can Wear Skirts, But You Have to Choose Wisely

Many women with heavy hips believe that they can't wear skirts at all. This is obviously a mistake, especially now that longer skirts are fashionable and easy to find. In fact, some of the most slimming looks around today are found in skirts and dresses. You have to be discriminating, of course. You should *never* wear dirndls, unpressed pleats, bulky wrap skirts, heavy woolens, most culottes, button-fronts that bag over the tummy and hips, and pencil-slim straight skirts. Nor is the swirling peasant skirt right, lovely though it may look on the skinny mannequins.

The advice we gave for disguising heavy legs also applies here: stick with darker colors, soft-to-clingy fabrics (jersey, lightweight wool, wool or cotton challis, *crêpe de chine*, soft cottons). The best styles are A-lines, stitched pleats in front with plain flared backs, and soft wraps (bias cut or four- to six-gore). Pair these skirts with silk or cotton blouses, cotton T's, and small fur sweaters, and the look takes off five to ten pounds.

If your waist is small and your bust is firm, one of the youngest, slimmest looks going today is a long-sleeved T tucked into (or belted over) a dark bias-cut calf-length skirt, worn with boots or dark-toned stockings and shoes. If further camouflage at the waist is needed, knot a blouse or light cardigan loosely over it, or wear a silk shirt hanging loose as an overblouse.

Rule Five: Patterns Will Work in Skirts, As Long As You Make Sure They Work for You and Not Against You

Solids are certainly more versatile and tend to stay in fashion longer. But *small* geometrics, florals or Art Deco designs on dark backgrounds, diagonal or vertical stripes (very slimming, both of these), or even small checks are good.

Avoid bright Day-glo colors such as fuchsia or orange or shocking pink, stiff or immoveable fabrics, dirndls, back-pocketed details, miniskirts, most culottes, shorts and hot pants, side-split pants and skirts, sheaths and "siren" looks or tight knits. These latter all cup the fanny and make you look strangely like a sausage out for a walk. Stay away, too, from short lengths and "nowhere" lengths—just at or over the knee. The former accentuates heavy hips and thighs. The latter, the "nowhere" lengths, make you look like a safe, dull and dowdy matron who can't make up her mind.

Now that the longer lengths are fashionable, wear them. They're fine camouflage and very elegant. Since lines must be kept simple, make the fabric, length and cut fashionable and contemporary and you'll manage to look devastatingly chic while you disguise your troublesome bottom at the same time.

FOR A THICK WAIST

Rule One: Avoid Anything That Cuts the Figure in Two, or Which Visually Adds Thickness or Bulk to the Waist

Stay away from extra-wide belts, especially the elastic cinch or lace-up variety. Ditto for dirndl and pleated skirts, scarf-wrapped waists, bare midriff looks, short-waisted dresses with cinched waists. Anything, in short, that focuses on the natural (and in this case, overweight) waistline. Instead, the trick is to create an "artificial waistline" or focal point elsewhere: just below the bust, or at the hip, for example.

Rule Two: If the Line Is Kept Simple and Straight, the Best Camouflage for the Waist Is Concealment

Given the variety of lovely tunic looks available today, along with the many cardigan sweaters, overblouses and vests, this is a relatively easy job. Some suggestions: a long thigh-length to knee-length slim tunic, for either day or evening; cardigans that skim the waistline or even wrap loosely; any slim-cut overblouse; a pullover sweater to wear over pants or skirts; an unbelted vest, poncho or jacket; even a long scarf that falls to the front and pulls the eye away from the waist-line.

Rule Three: Be Cautious with the Empire Waist

There are some extremely flattering Empire styles that are marvelous waist camouflage for fairly small-busted women. Large-breasted women beware: Empire waists give you a pouter pigeon look, or make you look six months pregnant. But an Empire dress on a woman whose only problems are hips and waist is often attractive. The same applies for the strapless "tube," either knotted or draped, if it really is a loose tube style and skims the waist area. The *slim* cut (not wide cut) chemise is fine too.

Rule Four: Always Match the Color or Tone of Your Belt with the Color or Tone of Your Skirt or Top

Narrow or medium-wide tailored belts are best. Avoid the wonderful bright peasant braids, gold metallic evening belts, belt bags, and wide sashes until the Bodysculpture routines begin to take effect. However, also bear in mind that a large striking belt buckle (the Alexis Kirk and Elsa Peretti silver buckles, for example, or an antique clip) can be a waist whittler on a small, narrow belt. It pulls the eye inward toward the middle and away from the sides. Try a large silver or ivory buckle on a thin belt that matches your costume, and you'll be startled at the results. Instant skinny!

A word of cheer: fortunately, the waist is probably the one area of most women's bodies which responds most quickly and favorably to exercise. With this in mind, we suggest that you spend relatively little money on waist disguises—certainly less than on camouflage for hips and leg problems, which are harder to overcome. At the beginning of your diet, you can simply wear T-shirts and sweaters pulled *over* pants and skirts instead of tucked in at the waist. If the outfit is a one-color or toned-in look, this can be surprisingly slimming: black turtleneck over black pants, rust cowled overblouse over rust pants. Knot blouses and even thin cardigan sweaters at the waist, and hide under shawls and shirtjackets a lot.

The main rule-of-thumb is: keep it simple and keep it all one color. A contrast at the waist, however subtle, draws attention to the problem spot. As for dresses, don't buy them until the inches have come off. But if you *must* have a dress, opt for a simple A-line, a straight-hanging princess style (no nipped-in waists), a simple wrap, or best of all, a tunic or chemise style. If the dress or top has a deep neckline—a V or deep button-placket style is excellent—all the better. The neckline lengthens your neck and face and gives the eye a new focal point. Fill in the neckline with silk neck cords, thin chains, delicate beads, strands of turquoise or coral, a filmy silk scarf (preferably a long one), and the camouflage is complete.

Legs, hips and waistline are the major problem areas that need camouflaging for 90 percent of women. But there are a few more problem areas that we ought not to neglect. Among these are upper arms, shoulders, back and neck areas. Many women seem to collect weight in these areas, and they can all be camouflaged successfully, as follows:

FOR HEAVY OR FLABBY UPPER ARMS

Here the secret is simple deception: cover them up. Or cover them at least partially, until the extra inches are gone. Arms, like waists, respond favorably to exercise, so that camouflage doesn't have to last long. For the time being:

Rule One: Avoid the Following: Strapless and Backless Styles, Sleeveless Dresses and Tops, Halters, Spaghetti Straps, Muscle-Sleeve T's and Other Bare or Short-Sleeve Styles

Rule Two: You Can Wear the Bell and Scarf-Type Gypsy Sleeves, Long, Three-Quarter Length, and

Elbow-Length Standard Sleeves

Small cap sleeves are flattering and pretty in the summer. The same goes for shawls, scarves, cardigan sweaters tied at the throat, or any other of a score of arm coverings.

As you begin to lose inches, you'll find, surprisingly, that the halter-style sleeveless top is more flattering than the standard sleeveless one—probably because it bares more shoulder and gives an added illusion of length to the arm. If you begin your routine in the summer when you have a light tan, look for a halter neck *maillot* or bikini. The halter *maillots* are particularly new and flattering, and especially if your back is tanned and moderately skinny, these suits shift the interest away from your arms to the long expanse of lean, tanned back.

FOR THE LARGE BUST

If your problem is a very large bust, there are two options: flaunting it or hiding it. For those who want the former, there is no problem. But if camouflage is desired . . .

Rule One: Avoid Anything That Accentuates the Problem Area

The best bets are V-necklines, loose button-front dresses, single-breasted dresses, coats, and blazers (avoid the double-breasted ones); draped or shirred bodices; crepe, jersey, and other soft materials; unfitted overblouses, if they are kept soft and fairly close to the body; open cardigans or vests; hip belts worn low with pants or skirts to move the natural waistline down a bit by optical illusion.

Rule Two: Be Sure That Your Bra Gives You the Support You Need

Buy the best bra for the money, which usually means one with a good bit of support. The no-bra or "braless" bras are nearly worthless support, but you aren't condemned to a life of Fiberfill and rubber inanities either. There are some attractive and clingy bras on the market today that offer the necessary support and are quite fashionable besides.

Rule Three: Avoid Looking Like You're Stuffed Into Your Clothes

Spend some money on alterations. Set-in armholes help, if they're well fitted. Don't let clothes look as if they're hanging from your shoulders.

Rule Four: There Are Items to Be Avoided

Stay away from Empire waistlines, starched/tailored men's shirts tucked into a skirt (especially if the blouse is buttoned at the neck), chemises (unless they have a good deal of flare at the hemline), minis and short-shorts, skinny-rib poor-boy jackets, the no-bra look, suspenders, fluffy, puffed sleeve blouses, the "peasant look," wide striped sweaters, and huge necklines.

Here are some other general recommendations on camouflage.

1. For generally heavy women, especially in the bottom half, avoid very narrow pencil-slim skirts (they accentuate *all* the figure faults), enormous cloaks or capes, long-haired fur jackets, any horizontally worked fur, wide collars, big hats, horizontal stripes, shawls with short skirts, flat heels with narrowish skirts, short stiff peplums, giant prints, and shiny satins.

2. Hair length is also important to the general proportion you're trying to achieve. Very long hair, attractive in a nymphettish sort of way on very young, thin girls, is a disaster on any heavy woman, regardless of her age. The best bet is a medium-length cut that varies from chin-length to collarbone-clearing length, depending on individual facial shape. A good blunt or slightly tapered cut is invaluable (can be worn up or down, made into a tiny bun or chignon for evening, curled or worn straight), and emphasizes the sought-after smaller proportions.

Contrary to popular belief, if your face is not positively balloon-shaped, there is no need to fear bangs. Side parted bangs or the newer, feathered ones are very flattering; so are slightly tapered layered cuts. So are small, neat knots, chignons, and neatly wrapped or turbaned heads. And while large hats should never be worn except possibly to the beach, small knit caps, soft little berets, soft fedoras, little brimmed caps and rainhats all are fine. All these can be very flattering, provided you have the proper hair-length and neat earrings and makeup. Out of the question are: teased heads, poufs, beehives, and shellac. The fat lady with her tons of pancake makeup and teased sausage curls is one recognizable cliché to be avoided like the plague it is.

3. Accessories should be chosen with care. You'll want to avoid huge oversized shoulderbags, itsy-bitsy evening purses, tight dog collars and/or chokers, the matronly one strand of pearls, jeweled harlequin glasses, pussycat bow-scarves, high buttoned collars—anything that breaks the line or accentuates the horizontal dimension.

Instead, lay on the vertical lines that are possible with long-lined scarves (silk or *crêpe de chine*), a medium-sized shoulderbag swinging from a long strap, a long envelope bag tucked under one arm, a thin silk neckring that just clears the collarbone, small silver and gold charms on shiny thin chains, a long fringed muffler looped over one shoulder, a tiny evening envelope of bronzed reptile or silk swinging from a long chain. Try out the accessories with the outfits you'll wear them with, remembering the basic rule of toning in colors carefully and stressing the vertical lines.

4. One rule of thumb on belts is worth repeating: an eye-catching buckle on a narrow leather belt can draw attention from the sides of the waist to the center. Alexis Kirk's copy of the basic Peretti "horseshoe" design is a good example: a thin leather ribbon attached to a medium-sized pewter buckle.

The most flattering leg-lengthening shoe is the one that leaves a long unbroken line at the ankle. The slingback, the pump, the wide-throated sandal, and the moccasin will all do nicely. Regardless of fashion's dictates, stay away from an absolutely flat heel and find a shoe with a heel at least an inch and a half to two inches high. The higher heels are certainly calf-lengtheners; nothing slims and lengthens a heavy leg quite like a graceful, higher-heeled shoe. Buy a suede or leather slingback, one pair of high-heeled moccasins for pants, and an evening sandal or slingback, and gradually expand as money and time allow.

5. Learn to avoid fussy, busy, overcomplicated designs and "thrown together" outfits. That means that you should steer clear of full or box-pleated skirts, patch pockets, plaids or widely contrasting colors; wide belts and wide-brimmed hats; horizontal trim; contrasting stockings, shoes, or boots; large puffed sleeves; bulky fabrics—tweeds, heavy wools, shiny satins, heavy velveteens, fluffy mohairs, heavy cottons, organdy, and felt. Seek out, instead, straight to slightly flared skirts; diagonal slash pockets; vertical stripes and solid colors; narrow belts; small caps; matching or toned-in stockings, shoes and boots; longer, tight-fitting sleeves. In fabrics, look for clingy materials that move—silk, crepe, jersey, chiffon, voile, thin, flat or fine-ribbed knits, wool challis, lightweight gabardine, synthetics like Qiana that move beautifully and are practically wrinkle-free; solids rather than patterns.

6. Don't forget that posture and carriage can work as camouflage. To begin with, practice walking tall with graceful, easy longish strides (think of Dina Merrill walking Borzois and Afghans through an autumn landscape). Borrow some tricks from professional models in standing and sitting. For example, don't face your audience (or the camera) head-on, hips facing straight. Instead, angle one hip slightly while standing and the effect is instantly slimming. If all that sounds confusing, stand in front of a mirror and angle the left hip toward the back, right hip toward the front, creating a slight and graceful S curve. If the classic model's pose looks stiff and contrived, try some different foot positions until one seems natural to you.

Sitting down, try crossing the legs high on the thigh and extending both slightly. Or placing one foot behind the other. Avoid sitting primly with two plump knees side by side—too oldladyish—or crossing at the knee, which makes the fat bulges reappear. Books like Peterson's *Photographic Modeling* can be a great help here. The same tricks the professional model uses to fool the camera can be used to fool a live audience. You don't want to make a fetish of all this—after all, no visual trick can substitute for real weight loss and toning through Bodysculpture—but you can certainly *appear* slimmer with these visual tricks.

7. Learn to think thin. There's a mind-set as well as a body-set that goes with being thin, and one that goes with being fat. While you're Bodysculpting, you're also shifting that mind-set.

Physicians and psychiatrists have known for a long time that fat people often continue to think of themselves as fat even when they're positively emaciated. The body image, in other words, doesn't change along with the actual body size.

Form a mental image of yourself as a thin person. If you've always been heavy, try blowing up a recent photo of yourself, then trimming away the fat with scissors. Hang the original and the doctored version on your refrigerator door.

Imagine yourself as you will be ten (twenty, thirty?) pounds lighter and three inches taller. Start moving, walking, standing as if you *were* that person. Imagine what you would wear; how you would sit, stand, bend. Wear clothes with a strong vertical line to help you maintain the image in your mind. A shoulderbag with a long strap, a long narrow muffler, a silk scarf with the ends swinging in front, long chains, a sweater-coat, tall boots. Do all your motions with this imaginary person (you in six months?) in mind, and you will start to make "thin" ways of moving a habit.

8. Don't forget the effect of properly applied makeup. The following optical illusions can be achieved in trying to make your face seem slimmer and recontoured.

—Slim and create shadows at the sides of the face and below the cheekbones by putting darker foundation (or dark brown pencil) at the hairline, the sides of the face and temples, and in the natural hollows of your cheeks. Blend this carefully with the lighter shade of your regular foundation (use liquid foundation for a youthful, moist look). Add a bit of cream rouge in the cheek hollows to accent them even more. Be careful to blend well: the aim is to get the merest suggestion of shadow or color, not a dark line of demarcation.

—To lengthen and slim your nose, use a darker foundation on the sides and a highlighter or gloss (perhaps a white or cream eyeshadow) down the bridge to the tip.

—Accent the cheekbones with gloss or highlighter across the tops of the bones themselves. Show off that new skeletal structure.

—Using a lip brush with a darker shade than your usual lipstick or gloss, outline the edges of your mouth. This trick emphasizes the mouth and gives it more definition, and in turn shapes and defines your face.

—Emphasize your eyes. If round eyes in a round face with round cheeks are a problem, lengthen or elongate your eyes into almond shape with liner and lashes. Experiment with "permanent" lashes, done either by you or by an expert, or feather-cut and tapered commercially made eyelashes. Or try the new eyelash strips which you can cut to your own specifications. Try various looks: upper and lower lashes, mascara on lower lashes, only deeper color in the crease, highlighting with cream or pastel shadow at the brow bone, watercolor-pale shadow, smoky or "kohl-colored" shadow, liner on, liner off. The looks are endless. Emphasizing the eyes—nearly everyone's best feature—calls attention away from chubby cheeks and squarish jawlines.

—Shade and contour an incipient double chin or sagging jawline in the same way cheeks are recontoured, with darker foundation blended into lighter. Make sure that the shading leaves no definite line. Tissue off excess foundation when you're done and double-check the results.

—Get a light suntan, either with Old Sol or with a sunlamp. Fortunately, getting burned to a crisp is no longer so fashionable, so an even, light overall golden tan is especially desirable. A *light* tan will make your face and body look pounds thinner. Keep it light, not only on your face but all over. Wear a big hat or at least a visor if you're in the sun for long periods of time. Supplement the natural color with blusher or a foundation with a light golden-bronze color like Clinique's Gold Rub.

9. Start developing an interest in fashion with a capital F. Not just what's In or Out this current season, but looks that are flattering, classic, elegant. Fat women, as a rule, are fashion dropouts. Bombarded by fashion magazines and store

windows with Size Two mannequins, stores with names like
The Smaller Than Small Shoppe or 5-7-9, they tune out the
Thin propaganda and learn to avoid small boutiques, makeup
counters, racks of fashion magazines, and the Saks catalogue
in the mail.

As you start noticing the good results of your Bodysculpture, you'll begin rediscovering the wonderful, colorful world
of clothes that you had tuned out (you thought) forever. Yes,
fashion can be frivolous, and narcissistic, but kept in proper
proportions, it can give you a healthy self-esteem and a new,
vital sense of feeling and looking good. While you're on your
Bodysculpture routine and diet, sharpen your eye and sense
of proportion. Window-shop. Brave the little boutiques that
intimidated you twenty pounds ago and try on something out-
rageous. Read catalogues and fashion magazines. People-
watch. Weed your wardrobe and pitch out the things that
make you look heavy. The Salvation Army and your heaviest
friends will love you. Become an expert in the looks that are
right for you.

10. Once you've weeded your wardrobe and gotten
down to within ten pounds of your ideal weight, start putting
together the Basic Four-part Camouflage Wardrobe. Start
looking for four pieces—pants, skirt, blouse, and cardigan
jacket or sweater—that work together. Since you're probably
starting virtually from scratch, why not make the four pieces
all one color? Try dark and light brown, navy, camel, black,
gray, or beige and taupe. Or build it around a two- or three-
color group: natural or white with beige and chocolate brown;
cream or ivory with gray or black; or navy and white with
deep wine or a claret shade. The fabric should be a lightweight seasonless fabric—lightweight gabardine or lightweight wool crepe, a thin knit, wool challis, and silk or *crêpe
de chine* for the blouse.

Build the wardrobe around simple, classic lines that provide
good camouflage: a soft, tailored shirt, softly flared, slim-cut
skirt; classic slim pants with only a suggestion of a flare at the
legs; thin, fanny-covering cardigan or jacket. Add a classic
raincoat or cape, a handsome thin luggage-colored belt, some
good jewelry (try a Peretti heart or teardrop, a silver or gold
cuff and an elegant pair of earrings for starters), silk scarves,

good leather boots and pumps or sandals, a classic leather shoulderbag or clutch, and you're ready to go.

The components of the four-part wardrobe can cost over $400 if they come from a European ready-to-wear line like Yves Saint Laurent, Cacharel, Sonia Rykiel, Ted Lapidus, or Missoni. About $250 will get you the same items in a good American designer line like Calvin Klein or Halston V. You might also try Oscar de la Renta Boutique, Beene Bag, Blassport, or Donna Karan for Anne Klein. Or look for some young, up and coming American designers like Carol Horn, Harriet Selwyn's Fragments, Cathy Hardwick, Clovis Ruffin, Cinnamonwear, or Jones New York, and find the whole thing for under $150.

The beauty of the wardrobe is that you can add to it season by season, year by year, until you have a whole coordinated look for every occasion. Next season, for example, add an extra cardigan, vest, or sweater, another skirt, or pants, a good wool coat. The following summer: a linen skirt and blazer or pants. Next fall: silk evening pants and a cashmere sweater or two.

Haunt sales for special items like a smashing bikini, a fringed evening shawl, a silk tunic, a jewel-tone dinner dress, a short fur jacket. Before long, you'll have not only the perfect figure but also the right wardrobe to complement it. You can camouflage whatever still needs hiding; flaunt your strong points, and generally show off the results of all those months of work.